GRESLEY'S
A3s

PETER TUFFREY

GREAT N-ORTHERN

ACKNOWLEDGEMENTS

Acknowledgements: I am grateful for the assistance from the following people: Roger Arnold, Ben Brooksbank, Doug Brown, David Burrell, Paul Chancellor, David Clay, Barry Cox, Marian Crawley, David Dunn, Peter Jary, David Joy, John Law, Hugh Parkin, Bill Reed, Andrew Warnes, Sue Warnes

Special thanks are due to my son Tristram for his help and encouragement throughout the project.

PHOTOGRAPHS

Unless otherwise stated, all photographs in this book are from the collections of either Malcolm Crawley or Ben Burrell. Every effort has been made to gain permission to use the images. If you feel you have not been contacted please let me know: petertuffrey@rocketmail.com.

INFORMATION

I have taken reasonable steps to verify the accuracy of the information in this book but it may contain errors or omissions. Any information that may be of assistance to rectify any problems will be gratefully received. Please contact me by email petertuffrey@rocketmail.com or in writing: Peter Tuffrey, 8 Wrightson Avenue, Warmsworth, Doncaster, South Yorkshire, DN4 9QL.

Great Northern Books Limited
PO Box 1380, Bradford, BD5 5FB
www.greatnorthernbooks.co.uk

Every effort has been made to acknowledge correctly and contact the copyright holders of material in this book. Great Northern Books Ltd apologises for any unintentional errors or omissions, which should be notified to the publisher.

ISBN: 978-0-9933447-6-3

Design and layout: David Burrill

CIP Data
A catalogue for this book is available from the British Library

CONTENTS

INTRODUCTION
BY DAVID JOY

At one time there were more A3s than just *Flying Scotsman*. Many more. The near hysteria surrounding the 2016 return to steam of this famous locomotive delighted the sceptics who were beginning to fear it would never happen. At the same time it tended to gloss over years long gone when it was just one of a class of 79. This book concludes with a look at its chequered career over the last half-century but is primarily a portrayal of the class as a whole.

The media frenzy surrounding *Flying Scotsman* featured what seemed to be a record number of half-truths and downright errors. The magnificent locomotive designed by Nigel Gresley was on countless occasions referred to as a train. It is not. Yet, there was a train of the same name and *Flying Scotsman* was just one of the locomotives that hauled it. Moreover, it was not originally an A3 class locomotive. It was an A1, although not even the first member of this class and definitely very different from the much later A1s built after the Second World War. Nor was it conceived by the London & North Eastern Railway [LNER] with which it came to be so closely associated. Small wonder that confusion reigns.

The evolution portrayed in these pages is that Nigel Gresley became chief mechanical engineer of the Great Northern Railway in 1911. He soon developed some superb locomotives leading in 1922 to the pioneer class A1 4-6-2 'Pacific', named *Great Northern* after the company and seen as the railway star of its age. A second A1 was promptly completed and ten more ordered. By the time these were built the Great Northern had in 1923 become part of the LNER and the first of the ten was also its first locomotive to be erected at the famous Doncaster Works. It was thus a natural choice to appear at the Wembley Exhibition in 1924 and to take the same *Flying Scotsman* name as had been given since the 1870s to the 10.0am express linking London with Edinburgh.

It was an early and successful example of the value of public relations, which was spectacularly eclipsed four years later. In 1928 it was decided that the Flying Scotsman express should henceforth make the longest non-stop run in the world with corridor tenders enabling a crew change to take place half-way through the 392-mile journey between the English and Scottish capitals. In business terms it might have been seen an irrelevant extravagance but not so to crowds thronging the lineside. It was inevitable that *Flying Scotsman* should be chosen to head the northbound train and near York it crossed sister locomotive *Shotover* hauling the non-stop from Edinburgh. There was today what would be termed massive media coverage, with the PR being skillfully manipulated to avoid mention that the 8¼-hour schedule was leisurely to the point of being slower than the Aberdeen fish train!

Gresley continued as chief mechanical engineer of the LNER and saw through the development of A1s into the A3s with improved valve settings, a higher boiler pressure and re-designed frames. The first production batch appeared in 1928 and they soon became known as 'Super Pacifics'. They were widely seen as not only the most elegant locomotive to have run on British rails but also fast, powerful and very economical.

A1s were gradually rebuilt as A3s but it was a process seen as desirable rather than urgent. *Flying Scotsman* was destined to be an A1 for another eleven years when in November 1934 it achieved the first fully authenticated 100mph speed on a British railway. It was nevertheless eclipsed only a few months later when the A3 *Papyrus* kept a four-hour schedule from King's Cross to Newcastle, and then back again, achieving a top speed of 108mph. The daily press had a field day, proclaiming that the LNER and Gresley had conquered the world.

This heyday coincided with the last eight A3s being erected at Doncaster Works. It was all a curtain raiser to the appearance in 1935 of the A4s, specially streamlined for high-speed running and henceforth stealing the limelight. Yet the A3s were still to be top-link locomotives for almost another three decades and retained their own special appeal for reasons that are not easy to define. It may in part simply have been a matter of looks, as their undoubted elegance managed to survive the later addition of double chimneys and smoke deflectors.

Another factor must surely have been their names. For all their supremacy, the streamlined A4s had a strange mixture and were named after wild birds, colonial dominions still reflecting the age of empire or, in near arrogance, directors of the LNER. Arguably much more attractive were the names of racehorses carried by virtually all the A3s. The choice was inspired, ranging from the gentle *Blink Bonny* and *Pretty Polly* through to the more racy *Flying Fox* and *Night Hawk*. Steam locomotives have always been termed 'she' by railwaymen, but this did not stop such names as *Dick Turpin* and even *Robert the Devil*.

The A3s certainly came to captivate the thousands collecting locomotive numbers and popularly known as 'train spotters' – a term that then embraced youngsters dutifully occupied rather than dismissed today as a questionable sub-species of humanity. This writer was one of them in the late 1950s, seeing hours spent on York station as far more rewarding than school homework. A3s could certainly not fail to be heard as they were heading lengthy expresses that stopped at a platform on a gentle curve and generally had great trouble in re-starting.

The driver would tug at the regulator handle and was eventually only too successful in getting steam into the cylinders. With a violent roar the chimney shot smoke and cinders skywards and the wheels slipped furiously, each point of contact tearing a flame of sparks from the rail. The safety valves roared and it was a memorable if deafening sight, with repeated attempts at forward progress sometimes lasting for almost five minutes.

It was a spectacle viewed as a matter of course by we number takers, who were more concerned with the challenge of how to see as many A3s as possible. The A4s remained in command and with luck it was possible to 'cop' all of them in a matter of months. They were shared between just three sheds on the East Coast main line and those at Edinburgh Haymarket, normally not working south of Newcastle, came through to London on the summer-only non-stop 'Elizabethan'.

In contrast, the A3s were scattered at ten sheds. Many were nevertheless a common sight at York, including *Flying Scotsman* allocated to King's Cross – always known simply as 'Top Shed' – and then seen as just one other express locomotive rather than something special.

The inescapable problem was that the greatest single allocation was at Edinburgh Haymarket, and these locomotives differed from the A4s in that they normally never ventured as far as York other than for the occasional major overhaul at Doncaster. At least they worked into Newcastle and the only way they could be seen with certainty was to spend precious pocket money and make-day visits to Tyneside.

More elusive still were *Sir Visto, Bayardo, Coronach* and *Flamingo* – the four A3s that in 1959 were allocated to Carlisle Canal shed. For a young lad in York, it involved major expeditions to Carlisle. Little excuse was needed when it gradually dawned that it was the only place in Britain where express 'Pacifics' of both LMS and LNER pedigree could be seen in a single station. It all proved too tempting, success with the A3s finally being achieved by getting out to Canal shed, a strange and inaccessible place different from the average with green grass and trees close at hand.

These four locomotives had their home in Carlisle to work services over the Waverley route to Edinburgh, passing through Border country that for many a mile had not a single habitation in sight. Its only equal in terms of remote surroundings was the Settle-Carlisle line, which provided a surprising swansong for A3s displaced from Gateshead shed by the advent of diesels. Sadly, few photographers got to see them as there was more activity on the West Coast main line at Shap.

By this time the steam age was in precipitous decline and *Prince Palatine* became the last A3 in regular service when it was withdrawn in January 1966. Three years earlier Alan Pegler had bought *Flying Scotsman* after it had covered over two million miles and its long stint at 'Top Shed' came to an end. He had the foresight to draw up a watertight contract with British Rail, guaranteeing operating rights when all other steam was banned. Quite what he was starting may not then have been apparent, but there can be no surprise that *Flying Scotsman* went on to achieve even greater fame if not fortune.

A final thought is that it could have been very different. A prime candidate for preservation ought to have been the pioneer A1 *Great Northern*, but Gresley's successor Edward Thompson was never forgiven for his rebuild of this important prototype. It was so unflattering that it has even been likened to putting a moustache on the Mona Lisa!

Above **No. 1470** *Great Northern*

Class A1 4-6-2 locomotive no. 1470 *Great Northern* (order no. 293 and works no. 1536) was completed at the Great Northern Railway's Doncaster 'Plant' Works on April 11, 1922. The locomotive is pictured in the area's New Erecting Shop on March 24, 1922. This was the result of Gresley attempting to provide an express passenger engine larger in size and with more power than the Ivatt wide firebox 'Atlantics'. It was Gresley's intention for the locomotives to haul trains weighing up to 600 tons. He reappraised the designs made in 1915 for a 'Pacific' or 4-6-2 engine in the light of the success of his three cylinder 2-6-0 and 2-8-0 locomotives. He also assessed the published information regarding proportions and proved steaming capacity of the Pennsylvanian Railroad K4 'Pacific' of 1911. Frames for the first A1, 1470 were laid in the New Erecting Shop on August 26, 1921. The engine was subsequently numbered 1470 and named before it left the Works. It was only the second GNR locomotive to carry a name. With a diagram 94 boiler, GNR 5,000-gallon tender and painted in GNR green, no. 1470 was allocated to Doncaster from new and remained there until July 8, 1944.

Opposite top left
No. 1470 *Great Northern*, boiler on hydraulic riveting machine at Doncaster Works, November 1921.

Opposite top right
No. 1470 *Great Northern*, frames in Doncaster Works' New Erecting Shop, November 1921.

Opposite below
No. 1470 *Great Northern*, boiler on frames, January 1922.

Above No. 1470 *Great Northern*
Photographed at Retford, no. 1470 *Great Northern*, still in GNR livery, underwent a Heavy repair between August 22, 1923 and October 9, 1923 and emerged with a livery of Apple Green with white lined boiler bands, black frames and cylinders with red lining.

Below No. 1470N *Great Northern*
Pictured on the King's Cross turntable, no. 1470N *Great Northern* carried the temporary LNER number, 1470N, between October 9, 1923 and March 21 1925. The engine was the only A1 not rebuilt to A3, departing from Doncaster Works, on September 25, 1945 as Class A1, later A1/1.

Above **No. 4472** *Flying Scotsman*

Following the building of nos 1470 and 1471 a second batch of ten A1s were ordered by the GNR and were constructed by the LNER (after absorbing the GNR) in 1923. No. 1472, was completed on February 7, 1923 and entered traffic 17 days later. The engine was the first to be erected at Doncaster after the Grouping of the railways. No. 1472 was renumbered 4472 on March 2, 1924 and named *Flying Scotsman* in the same year. Pictured in Doncaster Works Paint Shop, the engine is being prepared for the Wembley Exhibition of 1924. The engine was at Doncaster Works, December 27, 1923 to March 2, 1924. On the cab sides is the LNER's coat-of-arms which remained until 1928. No. 4472 was displayed on the LNER stand in the Palace of Engineering alongside Stockton & Darlington Railway No. 1 *Locomotion* of 1825. Also nearby was Great Western Railway Castle Class locomotive no. 4073 *Caerphilly Castle*. Visitors were said to be confused by a sign displayed near the GWR which said it was the most powerful locomotive in the UK. In the following year, exchange trials were made between the GWR and LNER comparing the running in traffic of Castle and A1 locomotives. As a result some modifications were made by Gresley to the A1s.

No. 1471 *Sir Frederick Banbury*

No. 1471 entered traffic from Doncaster Works (works no. 1539) on July 10, 1922 and was named *Sir Frederick Banbury* (the last chairman of the Great Northern Railway) on November 10, 1922. The frames had been laid for the engine at Doncaster on August 30, 1921. Working a test train of 600-ton tare between King's Cross and Barkston on September 3, 1922, no. 1471 gave an impressive performance, indicating the design was an important milestone for Gresley. Supplied with a 5,000 gal. GNR tender, no 1471's first allocation was to Doncaster, staying there until December 12, 1932. Renumbering to 1471N occurred on December 14, 1923 and then 4471 on August 1, 1925. Rebuilding to A3 was completed on October 16, 1942.

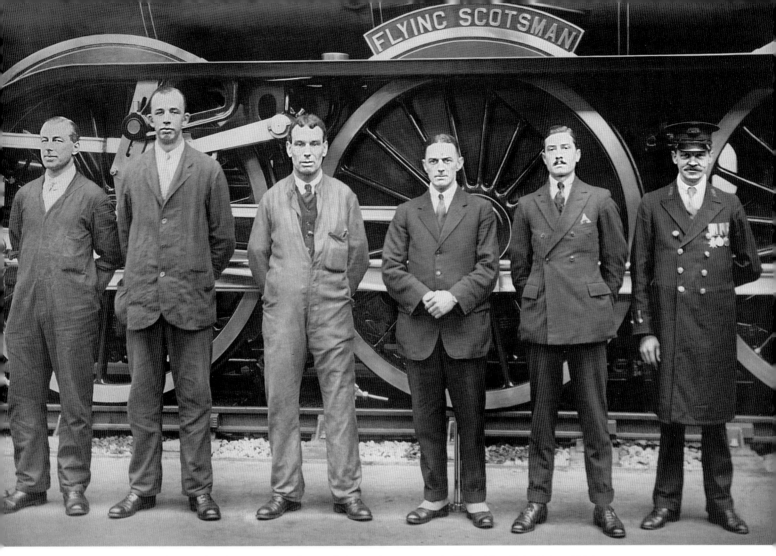

Above LNER staff pose for the camera in front of *Flying Scotsman* at the Wembley Exhibition, 1924.

Below **No. 4472 *Flying Scotsman***
No. 4472 is caught in a film break whilst shooting 'The Flying Scotsman' directed by Castleton Knight and which appeared in 1929. The black and white part-silent film was set on the London to Edinburgh 'Flying Scotsman' train and also featured the locomotive of the same name.

Above No. 1473 *Solario*

Starting its working life from Doncaster Works on March 17, 1923, no. 1473 was named *Solario* after Sir John Rutherford's 1925 Doncaster St Leger race winner. The engine was initially allocated to Doncaster and remained there until a move to Leeds Copley Hill during September, 1937. *Solario* was renumbered 4473 from June 14 1924 and long travel valves were fitted by December 1927. Rebuilding to A3 was carried out between August 22, 1941 and October 11, 1941.

Below No. 1474 *Victor Wild*

Named after the 1896 Kempton Park Jubilee Handicap winner, owned by T. Worton, no. 1474 *Victor Wild* was completed at Doncaster Works on March 24, 1923. Between August 14, 1929 and September 30, 1929 the locomotive was on Works to have long travel valves fitted. This followed successful tests carried out by Gresley's Technical Assistant Bert Spencer and the former gave instructions for all the Pacifics to be modified from May 1927.

Above No. 1476 *Royal Lancer*

Fronting an Up mail train at Ganwick is no. 1476 completed at Doncaster Works on May 26, 1923 and later named *Royal Lancer*. Initially allocated to Grantham, the engine was renumbered 4476 on February 7, 1925. Between December 23, 1927 and April 5, 1928 *Royal Lancer* underwent a General repair at Doncaster Works and re-entered traffic with a Diagram 94 boiler (no. 7647), corridor tender and long travel valves fitted.

Below No. 1478N *Hermit*

Waiting to depart from King's Cross is no. 1478N *Hermit* sent to traffic from Doncaster Works on June 30, 1923. Allocated to Doncaster from new and numbered 1478, the engine was renumbered 1478N on September 26, 1923 and 4478 on March 5, 1925.

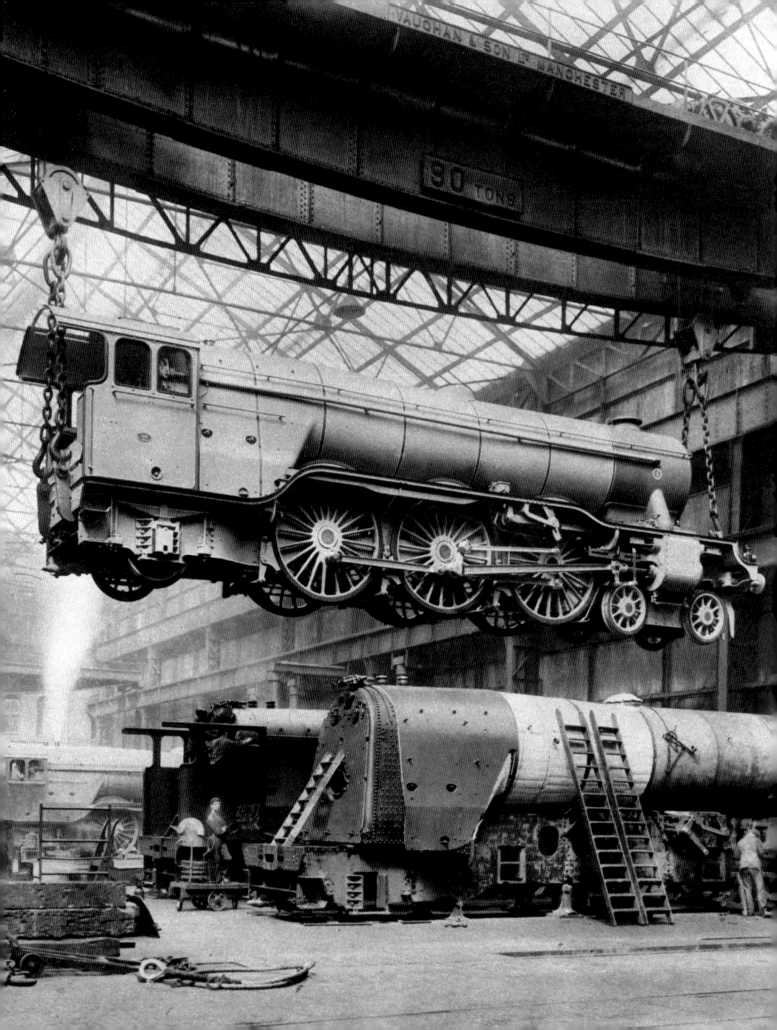

Above No. 2576 *The White Knight*

No. 2576 *The White Knight* went to traffic from the NBLC on October 19, 1924 with both vacuum and Westinghouse brakes. The engine was allocated to Gateshead when new; the Westinghouse pump was removed at Doncaster Works in July 1933. Departing from Edinburgh Waverley, the engine is working the up 'Flying Scotsman' train. The engine was named after the winner of the 1907 and 1908 Ascot Gold Cup. All but five, out of the total of 79 A1s/A3s, were named after racehorses. Names of racehorses began to be applied from April 1925. The *White Knight* was fitted with long travel valves at Darlington Works by June 1928 and altered to ACFI pump during April 1934. The latter was removed at Doncaster Works November/December 1938. Until May 1934, the engine was maintained at Gateshead Works, Darlington Works and Doncaster Works but afterwards solely at Doncaster Works (apart from a collision repair at Gateshead in March, 1951). Rebuilding to A3 was completed by July, 1943; adjustment to 75% cut-off, November 1956; double chimney and trough deflectors fitted, April 1959 and July 1961. During *The White Knight*'s existence two GNR 5,000 gal. tenders were attached, along with three LNER non-corridor tenders. Until rebuilding in 1943, five Diagram 94 boilers were supplied; then, five Diagram 94HP; and six Diagram 94A. Withdrawal was off St Margarets during July 1964 and scrapping at Arnott Young, Carmyle.

Opposite No. 2563 *William Whitelaw*

Twenty A1s were built at the North British Locomotive Company's Hyde Park Works, Glasgow between August 1924 and December 1924. Locomotive no. 2563, aloft on the crane, was the first to be completed and sent to traffic on July 9, 1924. Named *William Whitelaw* (*Tagalie* from August 2, 1941) the first allocation was Haymarket.

No. 4475 *Flying Fox*

A superb side view captures no. 4475 *Flying Fox* on the King's Cross station locomotive yard turntable. The engine was allocated new to the London shed from Doncaster Works on April 28, 1923. The 4475 number was applied on February 14, 1925 during a Doncaster Works' General repair visit. A GNR 5,000 gal. eight wheel tender – seen here –was carried until an LNER corridor one was attached following another General repair at Doncaster between June 2, 1928 and July 24, 1928. During this period the engine received Boiler no. 7699 (Diagram 94) and long travel valves were fitted.

Above No. 2549 *Persimmon*

No. 2549 (works no. 1605) went to traffic from Doncaster Works on October 25, 1924. The first allocation was to the town's shed, staying there until a move to Grantham on July 16, 1927. For a time the locomotive number was painted large in shaded numerals on the tender sides; it was also included in a small plate on each side of the cab. During a Doncaster Works' General repair, extending from May 27, 1927 until July 23, 1927, long travel valves were fitted. No. 2549 was eventually named *Persimmon* after the winner of the 1896 Derby and St Leger. The locomotive retained a GNR style tender throughout its working life. Rebuilding to A3 was from December 1943. A double chimney and trough deflectors were fitted during April, 1959 and October, 1961 respectively. Withdrawal was off New England during June, 1963.

Below No. 2562 *Isinglass*

No. 2562 *Isinglass*, (winner of the 1893 Derby, 2000 Guineas and St Leger), was in a batch of ten A1 locomotives ordered from Doncaster Works (order no. 302) during October 1923. The engine entered traffic on June 27, 1925 and was fitted with an 'E' type superheater following discussions between the New York office of The Superheater Co. and Gresley. This was intended to raise the steam temperature from the existing 575 degrees F., on the A1s in service, to 700 degrees F. Initially, two sets of the equipment were to be fitted on the P1s but instead one was fixed on no. 2562. Tests were subsequently made involving nos 2562 and 2570, the latter engine being equipped with an ordinary superheater. The results were not favourable for no. 2562 and the 'E' type superheater was replaced at Doncaster Works in August 1930 during a 44-day General repair. At the same time, long travel valves were fitted to the engine along with a Diagram 94 boiler (no. 7764).

No. 4474 *Victor Wild*

The engine was renumbered 1474N on December 14, 1923 and 4474 on November 15, 1925. Allocated to King's Cross from new, no. 4474, *Victor Wild* stayed there until removal to Doncaster on January 5, 1937. The engine is seen here on the King's Cross station locomotive yard turntable. During its working life the locomotive was attached to three GNR tenders and two LNER corridor tenders. Rebuilding from A1 to A3 was completed after a 53-day Heavy repair at Doncaster Works on October 1, 1942.

No. 2569 Gladiateur

No. 2569 *Gladiateur* was in a batch of 20 locomotives ordered from the NBLC (order no. L787) in December 1923. The engine was released to traffic on September 24, 1924 fitted with both vacuum and Westinghouse brakes (the latter apparatus was removed in January 1933). No. 2569 was also in the batch nos 2568-2582 that was equipped with Raven's fog signalling apparatus. Allocated to Gateshead from new, the engine remained there until a transfer to York on April 18, 1938. But, a return to Gateshead would be made a further six times.

No. 2544 Lemberg

No. 2544, *Lemberg*, completed at Doncaster Works on July 26, 1924, and allocated to Gorton, was one of two A1 locomotives (the other being 4480 *Enterprise*) first rebuilt to Class A3 in July and December 1927 respectively. This work included fitting the engines with a new higher pressure superheated boiler – increasing the pressure from 180 to 220 psi. The wide headers on the A3 boilers with parts projecting through the sides of the smoke box were covered with plates. Thus, these features were the main external differences between Class A3 and A1. Eventually, all but no. 4470 of the 52 A1s would be rebuilt to Class A3, the work extending to 1947. All new Pacifics built from 1928 were erected to the A3, instead of A1, specifications. At the same time as being rebuilt to A3, no. 2544 was also fitted with long travel valves.

No. 2543 *Melton*

Completed at Doncaster Works on June 28, 1924, no. 2543, *Melton* was the first A1 built with a chimney that was three inches shorter than on preceding members of the Class. This was to comply with North British loading gauge. Also, nos 2543 - 62 were amongst the first A1s to have 5¼ ins blastpipe orifices instead of 5½ ins. No. 2543 had long travel valves fitted by December 29, 1930 and was rebuilt to A3 in 1947.

Above **No. 2743 *Felstead***

The RCTS *Locomotives of the LNER Part 2A* points out there were two major differences between the earlier rebuilt A1s (to A3s) and the production A3s: 'The engines were fitted for left-hand drive and the cylinders were lined up to 19 in.' Moving the locomotive controls to the left hand side of the locomotive obviously put the driver in a more advantageous position for spotting signals. No. 2743 *Felstead* was amongst the first batch of production A3s – nos 2743 - 2752 – completed at Doncaster Works between August 1928 and April 1929. Entering traffic with a corridor tender on August 22, 1928, the engine was allocated to Doncaster shed, staying there until March 15, 1936.

Opposite **No. 2543, *Melton***

No. 2543, *Melton* was first allocated to Grantham (June 28, 1924) and then, before the end of the decade, had a number of stints at Doncaster. During one of these visits, c. 1927, it is likely the picture of the locomotive beneath the depot's coaling tower was taken. The image may have been intended to illustrate an article in *Popular Science Monthly* of August 1927 concerning the installation and operation of the then new coaling tower.

Below **No. 2744 *Grand Parade***

Ten corridor tenders were built for the first batch of production A3s nos 2743 - 2752 but only nos 2743, 2744 and 2745 received them. No. 2752 was allocated a corridor tender formerly attached to another engine; the rest were fitted with previously used GNR type tenders. No. 2744, *Grand Parade*, with corridor tender, was completed at Doncaster Works in August, 1928.

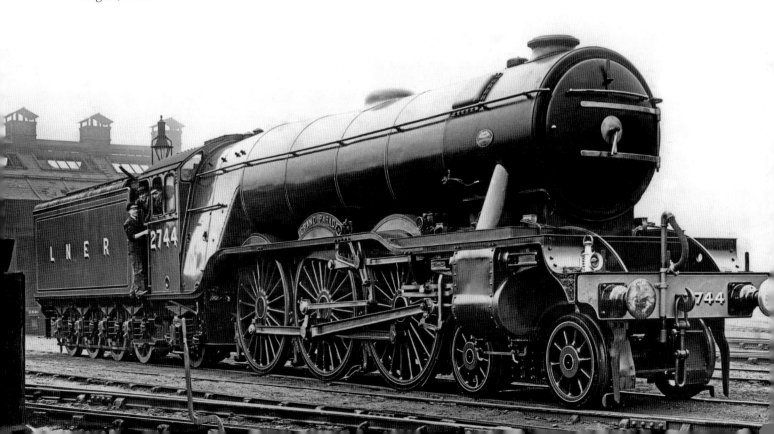

Opposite and above **No. 4472** *Flying Scotsman*

On May 1, 1928, the 'Flying Scotsman' train service was scheduled to run non-stop between King's Cross and Edinburgh for the first time. To announce details of the service the LNER took advertising space in most national daily newspapers. Perhaps an obvious choice to haul the train north out of King's Cross at 10 am was the appropriately named *Flying Scotsman* locomotive, no. 4472. Just after 6 pm, locomotive and train eased into Edinburgh Waverley station amidst loud cheers from hundreds of people including local dignitaries, railway officials, ordinary members of the public and excited schoolboys. It had successfully completed the 392 miles between London and Edinburgh without stopping, a record at the time for the LNER. The 1928 non-stop 'Flying Scotsman' had improved catering and other on-board services – even a barber's shop. On the same day, the non-stop 'Flying Scotsman' train from Edinburgh to London, which had left the Scottish capital at 10am was greeted with the same applause when it arrived at King's Cross. In fact, the greeting was so great that the LNER's welcoming party struggled to make their way through to the engine to praise the crew. Both train services used two sets of locomotive crew. For the first north-bound run, the engine was crewed by driver Pibworth and fireman Goddard on the southern section, with Messrs Blades and Morris of Gateshead taking over north of York. Inspector Brammall was assigned to accompany the crews. The relief crews accessed the locomotives from a carriage via the new type of corridor tender. Nigel Gresley rode part of the way on the King's Cross to Edinburgh train and accessed the corridor tender to chat with the engine's crew. The picture above shows no. 4472 *Flying Scotsman* about to leave King's Cross on May 1, 1928 with the inaugural non-stop run. The one opposite shows the *Flying Scotsman* locomotive and train at speed.

No. 2580 *Shotover*

Entering traffic from the NBLC on November 9, 1924, no 2580 was fitted with vacuum and Westinghouse brakes and allocated to Heaton from new. Named *Shotover* at Gateshead Works in October 1925, the engine was converted to A3 by February, 1928 and fitted with an LNER corridor tender by April 20, 1928. The corridor tender is clearly on display here, in a picture taken on May 1, 1928 when the engine hauled the first 'Flying Scotsman' non-stop train from Edinburgh to King's Cross. The corridor tender was removed by February 27, 1929 and the engine, for the rest of its working life, was attached to a GNR type tender. The Westinghouse pump was removed in 1934.

Above No. 2548 *Galtee More*

Pictured being lifted back on to its wheels in the Doncaster Works' Crimpsall repair shops during July 1930 is no. 2548 *Galtee More*. The locomotive entered Works on May 20, 1930 for a General repair and a change of boiler, leaving on July 5, 1930. Originally built at Doncaster Works and entering traffic on September 27, 1924, no 2548 was initially allocated to Grantham and was to return there on five more occasions. Long travel valves were fitted by October 18, 1928 and conversion to A3 did not occur until October 1945. *Galtee More* carried a GNR 5,000 gal. tender throughout its working life.

No. 4472 *Flying Scotsman*
No. 4472 *Flying Scotsman* is undergoing repairs in the Doncaster Works Crimpsall repair shops 4-bay. The locomotive was maintained at Doncaster throughout its working life.

Above **No. 2570** *Tranquil*

Emerging from the NBLC on September 27, 1924 with vacuum and Westinghouse brakes, no. 2570 *Tranquil* was fitted with long travel valves on December 20, 1927 and the latter alteration may be spotted here. The Westinghouse pump was removed during October 1933 and rebuilding to A3 was not completed until October 1944. The engine was allocated to Gateshead from new and returned there on seven occasions. There were also five allocations to Darlington and one each to York (North), Neville Hill and Heaton. Throughout its working life the engine was attached to a GNR 5,000 gallon tender. Repair work was carried out at Doncaster (Heavy, General and Light), Darlington Works (General and unclassified) and Gateshead (Light). As mentioned previously, in the caption for no 2562, no 2570 underwent superheater comparison tests with the former locomotive in 1926.

Above No. 2546 Donovan
No. 2546 *Donovan* was a Doncaster Works-built A1 and during its working life the engine had 18 allocations including King's Cross, Copley Hill (Leeds), Doncaster, Grantham and New England. Pictured with an LNER corridor tender, this was only carried for four days in May 1928. Long travel valves were fitted from December 1927 and rebuilding to A3 was completed by January, 1948.

Opposite above No. 2751 Humorist
No. 2751 *Humorist* was built, as an A3, at Doncaster Works and entered traffic on March 7, 1929. The first allocation was Doncaster shed. The engine is pictured there around March 1933 with the top of the smokebox cut away and wind vanes fitted. This work was part of Gresley's smoke lifting experiments involving the engine. Eventually a successful outcome was gained but none of the other Pacifics were altered. Also, in spite of the time spent on the experiments, no. 2751 reverted to its 'normal' appearance in January 1934 but a double chimney was fitted from July 1937.

Opposite below No. 2560 Pretty Polly
The engine – seen here travelling at speed – entered traffic as an A1 from Doncaster Works in April, 1925. The first allocation was to Gorton for just over a month before a transferral to King's Cross. In total the engine would have 17 allocations. Doncaster Works took care of maintenance throughout the engine's working existence and this included fitting long travel valves from January 1930. *Pretty Polly* was rebuilt to A3 from May 1944 and up to this point the engine was supplied with five different Diagram 94 boilers.

Above **No. 2598** *Blenheim*
Pictured in the Doncater Works New Erecting Shop on September 12, 1936 is no. 2598 *Blenheim*. Whilst having a General repair, the engine also underwent centre of gravity experiments with an empty boiler. Scribed lines on the lifting plate show the difference between an empty and full boiler. *Blenheim* was built as an A3 at Doncaster Works during June, 1930.

Opposite above **No. 2596** *Manna*
Receiving admiring glances from staff at Newcastle Central station is no. 2596 *Manna*, turned out as an A3 from Doncaster Works on February 22, 1930. Allocated to Gateshead from new, the engine returned there on two more occasions; two stints were also noted at Heaton. *Manna* was supplied with five tenders: four LNER non-corridor; and one GNR type. Newcastle station, built to the designs of John Dobson (1787-1865) was formally opened by Queen Victoria on August 29, 1850. Photograph reproduced courtesy of J.W. Armstrong Trust collection.

Opposite below **No. 2596** *Manna*
Another view of no. 2596 *Manna* shows the engine approaching Arksey, north of Doncaster, at walking pace with the up 'Flying Scotsman' during extreme floods in South Yorkshire on June 3, 1932. Photograph from the David Joy collection.

Above No. 2579 Dick Turpin

No. 2579 *Dick Turpin* entered traffic from the NLBC on November 3, 1924 with both vacuum and Westinghouse brakes and was allocated to Heaton shed (in existence between 1875 - 1963). By the close of 1924, Heaton would have five A1s allocated, nos 2578, 2579, 2580, 2581, 2582. Works visits for no. 2579 were at Gateshead and Darlington until 1931 then, with the exception of two visits to Darlington in 1935 and 1964, the locomotive was maintained at Doncaster Works. The engine was named *Dick Turpin* at Gateshead Works during a short visit there between October 23, 1923 and October 27, 1925.

Opposite above No. 2750 Papyrus

No. 2750 *Papyrus* was posed for this picture with the dynamometer car and train after breaking the world speed for steam traction. This occurred on an Up run between Newcastle and King's Cross, on the Little Bytham - Essendine section, on March 5, 1935. The locomotive's speed peaked at 108mph before Essendine. The crew for the record run were driver Bill Sparshatt and fireman Webster. No. 2750 was built as an A3 at Doncaster Works and entered service on February 23, 1929 being allocated initially to King's Cross. Between 1929 and 1953, the engine's tender was changed on no fewer than 10 occasions.

Opposite below No. 2746 Fairway

Built as an A3 at Doncaster Works and entering traffic on October 26, 1928, no. 2746 *Fairway* was allocated to King's Cross, staying there until a short transfer to Gateshead on November 10, 1936. The locomotive was attached to four tenders: one GNR type; two LNER non-corridor; and one streamlined non-corridor. *Fairway* is pictured here on a Cowans & Sheldon turntable.

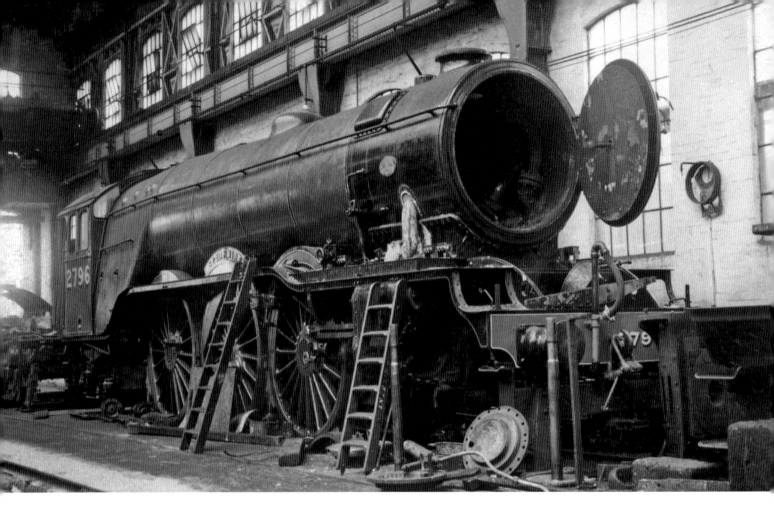

Above **No. 2796 *Spearmint***

No 2796 *Spearmint* is located at the east end of 4-Bay in the Doncaster Works Crimpsall repair shop. Dating from around 1901, the large shop was situated to the west of the main works buildings and many of the Pacifics received General repairs in that area. No. 2796 entered traffic from Doncaster Works as an A3 on May 17, 1930 and was allocated north of the border for all its working life.

Below **No. 2500 *Windsor Lad***

No. 2500 *Windsor Lad*, pictured at Doncaster Works when new, entered service from there as an A3 during July, 1934. The engine was in the batch of the last eight A3s erected. It retained the same LNER non-corridor tender throughout its working life and allocations were to Scottish sheds. With the exception of light repairs carried out twice at Cowlairs during 1941 all other work was at Doncaster.

Above No. 2547 *Doncaster*
Entering traffic from Doncaster Works as an A1 on August 30, 1924, no. 2547 *Doncaster* accelerates through Holloway on the 'Flying Scotsman' service. The locomotive is perhaps pictured during one of two periods in 1928 when it was attached to a corridor tender.

Below No 2566 *Ladas*
No. 2566 *Ladas*, built by the NBLC, and entering traffic on August 14, 1924, was allocated to Scottish sheds – Haymarket (twice), Dundee Tay Bridge, Eastfield and St Margarets – until 1940. Tablet apparatus, as may be detected here, was fitted during a 35-day visit to Cowlairs between June 6, 1930 and July 10, 1930. The engine was rebuilt to A3 by November 4, 1939.

Above **No. 4476** *Royal Lancer*

No. 4476 *Royal Lancer*, hauling an unidentified train, was rebuilt to A3 after a 56-day General repair at Doncaster Works from October, 1946. The engine was adjusted to 75% cut off in 1948; and converted from right hand to left hand drive from December, 1952.

Below **No. 2568** *Sceptre*

Built at the NBLC, no. 2568 *Sceptre* went to traffic in September, 1924 with both vacuum and Westinghouse brakes (the latter removed by February 1933). The first allocation was to Gateshead, remaining there until December, 1936. Long travel valves were fitted at Darlington Works from December 1927. *Sceptre* is seen at speed on March 18, 1930.

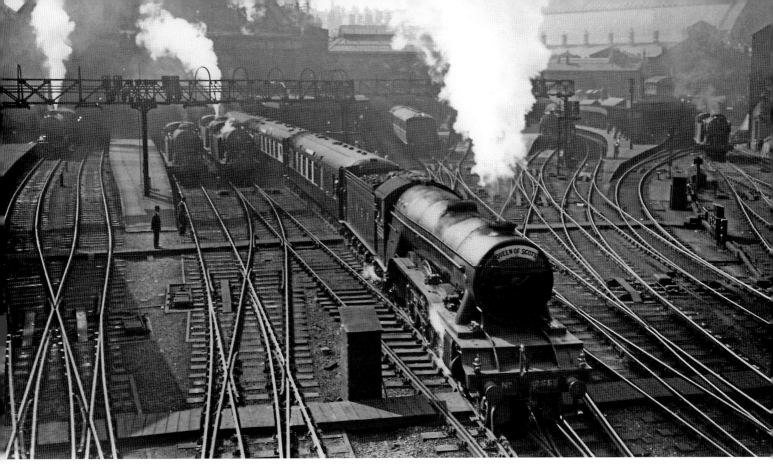

Above No. 2555 *Centenary*
No. 2555 *Centenary* eases the 'Queen of Scots' Pullman train out of King's Cross. Operating between London and Glasgow Queen Street, the train ran via Leeds Central and Harrogate, 1927 - 1939 and 1948 - 1978.

Below No. 4475 *Flying Fox*
No. 4475 *Flying Fox* is at King's Cross in June 1938. Photograph courtesy of J.W. Armstrong Trust.

Above No. 2744 *Grand Parade*

No. 2744 *Grand Parade* is on the south side of the Crimpsall repair shop at Doncaster Works during April 1938 following involvement, in the Castlecary station accident. This occurred around 4.37pm on Friday December 10, 1937 and left 35 dead and 179 injured. In heavy snow, no. 2744 was hauling the 5.30pm down express train, Edinburgh Waverley to Glasgow Queen Street and overran the home signal at danger. It collided at speed, about 60mph, with the rear of the preceding 2.00pm down express train from Dundee Tay Bridge to Glasgow Queen Street. The latter train hauled by Class D29 4-4-0 locomotive no. 9896 *Dandie Dinmont* was standing just beyond the station platform. Quite remarkably the driver and fireman of *Grand Parade* had lucky escapes with slight injuries. But the driver of the other train received severe injuries having been thrown from the footplate. No. 2744 *Grand Parade* was subsequently rebuilt.

Opposite No. 2582 *Sir Hugo*

The NBLC built no. 2582 *Sir Hugo* as an A1 and it was in service from December, 1924. Long travel valves were fitted in February 1930 and the engine was rebuilt to A3 by December 17, 1941. *Sir Hugo* is at Grantham during August 1946 after spending 64 days undergoing a General repair at Doncaster Works. During that time, the engine lost its wartime unlined LNER Black livery and was repainted in Apple Green with white lined black boiler bands, black frames and cylinders with red lining. Between May 28, 1949 and September 2, 1952 it was painted BR Blue with black and white lining. Photograph courtesy of Colourrail.

Above **No. 92 *Fairway***

During the LNER's post-war locomotive renumbering schemes, no. 2746 *Fairway* was initially numbered 555 but this was not applied. Between October 27, 1946 and April 13, 1949 the number carried was 92. The locomotive is seen here with the latter number at King's Cross on February 12, 1948. This was subsequently changed to 60092. The locomotive was maintained throughout its working life at Doncaster Works and the work included adjustment to 75% cut-off, December 1953; fitting of double chimney and trough deflectors, November 1959 and October, 1961. Withdrawal was off Gateshead during October, 1964.

Opposite above **No. 2559 *The Tetrarch***

York engine shed, comprising four turntables, is seen after the Luftwaffe attacked the city on the night of April 29, 1942. One hundred and nine people died in the raid with over 200 injured. The shed was holding around 50 locomotives and when a 500kg bomb landed (in no. 4 shed) a number of them were seriously damaged. This included Class A4 4-6-2 engine no. 4469 *Sir Ralph Wedgwood* which was subsequently scrapped. Pictured is locomotive no. 2559, *The Tetrarch* built at Doncaster Works and entering service on March 28, 1925. The engine was rebuilt to A3 specifications in January 1942 – only a few months prior to the York raid. Picture reproduced courtesy of Simon Lathlane.

Opposite below **Nos 513, 2872, and 107 *Royal Lancer***

Thompson A2 4-6-2 locomotive no. 513 *Dante* (built May 1944); and B17 4-6-0 locomotive no. 2872 *West Ham United* stand at King's Cross shed alongside no. 107 *Royal Lancer*. The latter engine carried the LNER 1946 second number – '107' – from October 4, 1946. Renumbering to 60107 occurred on April 23, 1948. The locomotive was allocated to King's Cross shed between May 19, 1946 and June 4, 1950.

Above No. 86 *Gainsborough*

No. 86 *Gainsborough* was built as an A3 and entered service on April 7, 1930. It is travelling near Burnmouth with a Down express on August 25, 1947. Earlier in May of that year, and after a 31 day General repair, the engine was repainted from wartime unlined LNER Black to Apple Green. On September 16, 1948 the BR number 60086 was applied and from May 13, 1949 another repaint would see the engine in BR Blue livery, lasting until June 18, 1952. Apart from a 14 day Light repair at Darlington Works in 1935, *Gainsborough* was maintained entirely at Doncaster Works. Allocations took the engine no further south than Doncaster and it was attached to only one LNER non-corridor tender – no 5478 – throughout its existence. The engine was withdrawn from Neville Hill during November 1963.

Opposite above No. 56 *Centenary*

The engine emerged from Doncaster Works on February 7, 1925 as an A1, numbered and named 2555 *Centenary*. The LNER 1946 second number was applied on July 10, 1946 whilst the engine was allocated to Doncaster; a move to King's Cross occurred on October 27, 1946. BR number 60056 was added on May 18, 1949. A GNR 5,000 gal. tender was carried throughout the locomotive's working life.

Opposite below No. 105 *Victor Wild*

No. 105 *Victor Wild* is at New Southgate on July 12, 1947 with the Down 18.05 King's Cross to Leeds and Bradford. The engine held the LNER 1946 second number – 105 – between May 12, 1946 and August 18, 1948, eventually becoming BR 60105. Conversion from right hand to left hand drive was carried out by February 20, 1953. During 1939 *Victor Wild* was allocated once to Leicester and twice to Gorton but at the time of the photograph was a King's Cross engine. A double chimney was fitted by March, 1959, and trough deflectors, December 1960. As 60105, *Victor Wild* was condemned at Grantham during June, 1963.

Above **No. 60065** *Knight of Thistle*
Completed at the NBLC in July 1924, no. 60065 *Knight of Thistle* was originally named *Knight of the Thistle*. Renaming to *Knight of Thistle* occurred on December 28, 1932. Fitting of long travel valves was from June, 1928, and until April 1931 the engine was maintained exclusively at Cowlairs. Rebuilding to A3, was carried out at Doncaster Works by March, 1947. The BR Blue livery with black and white lining was applied between November 18, 1949 and December 24, 1952. From the latter date the locomotive was converted from right to left hand drive. Photograph of the locomotive at Edinburgh Haymarket shed in 1949, reproduced courtesy of Colourrail.

Opposite above **No. 60043** *Brown Jack*
No. 60043 *Brown Jack* is carrying the BR number that was applied from August 11, 1948 and this photograph at Edinburgh Waverley was taken around that time. Built as an A3 and entering service from Doncaster Works (as no. 2508) on February 9, 1935, *Brown Jack* was allocated to Haymarket. Staying there until November 6, 1961, the engine then moved to St Margarets. Apart from a 52-day unclassified visit to Cowlairs in 1962, no. 60043 was repaired throughout its existence at Doncaster Works.

Opposite below **No. 60110** *Robert the Devil*
No. 60110 *Robert the Devil* is at Potters Bar Tunnel with the 16.05 to Grantham and Lincoln on May 7, 1949. Entering traffic as an A1 from Doncaster Works in June 1923, the engine was rebuilt to A3 at the same location during August, 1942. Conversion to left hand drive was undertaken by January 2, 1953. Apple Green livery was applied between February 8, 1947 and August 3, 1950.

Above No. 60046 *Diamond Jubilee*

No. 60046 *Diamond Jubilee* hurries past Wortley South Junction during October 1951 with 'The White Rose'. The engine is in BR Blue livery which had been applied on August 5, 1949. Conversion from right hand drive to left hand drive was undertaken during a 37-day Heavy Intermediate repair at Doncaster Works, that was completed on October 29, 1952. During this works visit no. 60046 was also painted in Brunswick Green. At the time of the photograph the engine was allocated to Doncaster. Photograph courtesy of *Yorkshire Post Newspapers*.

Opposite above No. 60041 *Salmon Trout*

No. 60041 *Salmon Trout* is at Grantshouse with an Up express on August 13, 1949. The engine went into service as an A3 from Doncaster Works on December 19, 1934 and was allocated to Haymarket where it remained until July 13, 1960. *Salmon Trout* is in Apple Green livery which was applied on May 7, 1947 and remained until July 7, 1950 when repainted BR Blue. Brunswick Green would be applied from February 1952.

Opposite below No. 60083 *Sir Hugo*

No. 60083 *Sir Hugo* is reversing at Leeds City station on December 12, 1952. The engine was only allocated to two sheds throughout its working life: Heaton, December 6, 1924 to June 17, 1940; Gateshead until October 26, 1940; Heaton to June 16, 1963; Gateshead until withdrawal. Photograph courtesy of *Yorkshire Post Newspapers*.

Above **No. 60112** *St Simon*
Pictured in BR Blue at Leeds Central station on October 17, 1951, no. 60112 *St Simon* is about to embark on a journey to
King's Cross. The engine emerged from Doncaster Works with no. 1481N on September 8, 1923. Renumbering to 4481
occurred on August 1, 1925. The first allocation was to Doncaster where the engine was to return on a further eight
occasions. *St Simon* was rebuilt to A3 at Doncaster Works by August 30, 1946, after a 56-day Heavy repair. At the time of
the photograph the locomotive was allocated to Grantham. Conversion from right to left hand drive was carried out by
October 24 1952; a double chimney added from July, 1958; and trough deflectors, October 5, 1962 after an 80-day General
repair. Apart from a brief period 1937/1938 when the engine carried a streamlined non-corridor tender, five GNR 5,000
gal. tenders were attached during its working life.

Opposite above **No. 60074** *Harvester*
No. 60074 *Harvester* is running through the Neville Hill area with a freight train during the 1950s. Built at Doncaster
Works and entering traffic on October 8, 1924, *Harvester* was rebuilt to A3 from April 17, 1928. At the time of the picture
the engine was allocated to Leeds Neville Hill (December, 17 1950 to April 8 1963). During a 32-day General repair at
Doncaster Works, completed on November 6, 1952, no. 60074 emerged converted from right hand to left hand drive and
painted in Brunswick Green. Further alterations would see the locomotive have 75% cut off (from January 6, 1956) and a
double chimney fitted (from March 20, 1959).

Opposite below **No. 60077** *The White Knight*
No. 60077 *The White Knight* is at Leeds. Photograph by Eric Treacy from David Joy collection.

Above **No. 60064** *Tagalie*

No. 60064 *Tagalie* (formerly *William Whitelaw*) is on 'standby' just south of Doncaster station and adjacent to the ECML on March 27 1952. Gazing down from Hexthorpe Bridge to view the 'standby' engine was a regular treat for train-spotters in the early 1960s; the duty usually allocated to an A3, A1 or V2. The engine was allocated to Scottish sheds until removing to Doncaster on July 2, 1950 and staying there until June 14, 1959. Withdrawal from Grantham was on Monday September 4, 1961. Photograph courtesy of *Yorkshire Post Newspapers*.

Opposite below **No. 60053** *Sansovino*

No. 60053 *Sansovino* was built as an A1, emerging from Doncaster Works in December 1924 and allocated to King's Cross, the first of 17 allocations during the engine's service history. Doncaster Works took care of all the maintenance and alterations: long travel valves were fitted by February 1928; and rebuilding to A3, June, 1942. *Sansovino* carried all four possible numbers: LNER (1924), 2552; LNER (1946 1st), 521, from March 1946; LNER (1946 2nd) 53, from November 1946; and BR, 60053, from February 1949. Five different GNR tenders were attached; one LNER corridor tender; and one LNER non-corridor tender. Adjustment to 75% cut off was done by February 1957; and a double chimney fitted, November 1958. Withdrawal was off Heaton at the end of May 1963 and cutting up at Doncaster Works. *Sansovino* is at Brookmans Park with an Up train on September 8, 1951.

Previous pages **No. 60055** *Woolwinder*

Heading the 15.20 service to King's Cross at Copley Hill, Leeds on August 1, 1952 is 60055 *Woolwinder* in Brunswick Green livery applied in November of the previous year. Built at Doncaster as no. 2554 on December 31, 1924 the engine's first allocation was to the town's shed where it was to return on two further occasions. There were four allocations to Grantham and three to King's Cross. Between August 18, 1939 and November 22, 1942 the engine was allocated to Gorton. A stint at Leeds was recorded between October 2, 1943 and December 16, 1944. After involvement in a collision in Marylebone tunnel in 1941, the locomotive was repaired over a 17-day period at Doncaster Works. Rebuilding to A3 occurred in the following year and a double chimney was added in 1958. Five different GNR 5,000 gal. tenders were attached to *Woolwinder* during its working life. Photograph courtesy of *Yorkshire Post Newspapers*.

Above No. 60081 *Shotover*

Heading for London, with the 'Queen of Scots' Pullman train, no. 60081 *Shotover* passes through Weeton and Huby, with Almscliff in the background, on May 16, 1952. The train service ran between Glasgow Queen Street- London King's Cross via Harrogate and Leeds Central, 1927-1939 and 1948-1978. At the time of the photograph *Shotover* was allocated to Leeds Neville Hill (February 6, 1949 - October 1, 1962) from where it was withdrawn. Cutting up was at Doncaster Works from May 28, 1963. Photograph *Yorkshire Post Newspapers*.

Above **No. 60060** *The Tetrarch*

During November 1951, no. 60060 *The Tetrarch* eases out of Newcastle station, originally titled Newcastle-on-Tyne Central. The panoramic view shows the eastern approach to the station from the castle. *The Tetrarch* entered traffic from Doncaster Works on March 28, 1925 and was allocated to Gorton for a month before moving to King's Cross. From March 9, 1939 the engine remained in the north east until withdrawal. Photograph courtesy of *Yorkshire Post Newspapers*.

Opposite above **No. 60094** *Colorado*

Doncaster Works completed the erection of the engine as an A3, no. 2748, during December 1928 and apart from two Light repairs at Cowlairs, in 1940 and 1944, carried out all its major maintenance and alterations. Adjustment to 75% cut-off was from September 1947; renumbering to 60094, December 1948; fitting a double chimney and trough deflectors, August 1959 and August 1961 respectively. Attached during the service life were three GNR type tenders and one LNER non-corridor tender. Withdrawal was from St Rollox on Monday February 24, 1964 and the engine was subsequently sold for scrap to Hendersons of Airdrie. Photograph of *Colorado* at Grantshouse, working a Down fitted freight on June 20, 1953, by J. Robertson.

Opposite below **No. 60040** *Cameronian*

No. 60040 *Cameronian* pauses between duties at the east end of Edinburgh Haymarket shed on April 11, 1957. The first Haymarket shed was built in 1842 and situated at the north end of Haymarket station. A second shed was erected just over half a mile away from the earlier one in 1894. Entering traffic from Doncaster Works as an A3, no. 2505, the engine was allocated to Haymarket. Apart from a brief stay at York (North) in 1939, the engine spent its entire working life allocated to North East sheds. Photograph by Bill Reed.

Above No. **60067** *Ladas*

Renumbered 60067 on July 30, 1948, *Ladas* is parked at the north end of Doncaster shed during the 1950s. The original engine shed at Doncaster was located at the town's station with space for thirty locomotives. Doncaster Carr shed was opened in 1876, about a mile south of the town's station, and with two coal stages. Costing around £37,000, the shed was 420ft by 180ft and equipped with twelve roads open at each end. There was space for up to 100 locomotives and a mechanical coaler was installed around 1926. Closure to steam occurred in May 1966. Photograph by Bill Reed.

Opposite above No. **60074** *Harvester*

No. 60074 *Harvester* hauls The Queen of Scots' Pullman past Arthington North Box in June 1959. Initially, the locomotive was fitted with both vacuum and Westinghouse brakes; the latter removed from March 1935. Gateshead Works, Darlington Works and Doncaster Works were all involved with the engine's maintenance; Doncaster Works exclusively from December 1936. *Harvester* was withdrawn off Leeds Neville Hill during April, 1963. Cutting up was undertaken at Doncaster Works. Photograph reproduced courtesy of *Yorkshire Post Newspapers.*

Opposite below No. **60071** *Tranquil*

The Bramhope tunnel was constructed, on the Harrogate line, between 1845-1849 and is noted for its crenellated north portal and for the deaths of 24 men during its construction. The latter is commemorated in Otley churchyard with a castellated replica of the north portal. No. 60071 *Tranquil* runs into Arthington from Bramhope tunnel in June 1957. A double chimney was added by July 1958 and trough deflectors, November 1961. The engine spent much of its working life allocated to Gateshead shed (eight times) from where it was withdrawn on October 12, 1964. In December 1964, it was sold for scrap to A. Draper, Hull. Photograph courtesy of *Yorkshire Post Newspapers.*

Above **No. 60085** *Manna*

Working along the old Leeds & Selby railway line (opened in 1834) no. 60085 *Manna* is in Marsh Lane Cutting, approaching Leeds, whilst heading a Newcastle-Liverpool express on November 15, 1951. Upper Accommodation Road is running above the locomotive with lines to the left leading to a goods station, formerly the Leeds & Selby railway station. The tunnel here was formerly much longer until opening out in 1894. *Manna* was painted in Brunswick Green from December 23 1952; adjusted to 75% cut off June, 1957; a double chimney and trough deflectors fitted from November 5, 1958 and April 27, 1962. Withdrawal from Gateshead was during October, 1964 and in December of the same year *Manna* was sold for scrap to A. Draper, Hull. Photograph courtesy of *Yorkshire Post Newspapers*.

Opposite above **No. 60070** *Gladiateur*

Photographed during the 1950s alongside the old north coal stage at Doncaster shed is no. 60070 *Gladiateur*. Rebuilding to A3 was completed during July, 1946; conversion to left hand drive, July 3, 1953; a double chimney and trough deflectors fitted, April, 1959 and September, 1961 respectively. Between March 2, 1943, and withdrawal from Gateshead on Monday May 4, 1964 *Gladiateur* was attached to two different LNER non-corridor tenders. Scrapping was carried out by A. Draper of Hull from July 1964. Photograph by Bill Reed.

Opposite below **No. 60041** *Salmon Trout*

No. 60041 *Salmon Trout* is beside the mechanical coaler at Haymarket during the 1950s. Adjustment to 75% cut-off was completed by October, 1956. A double chimney was fitted from July 31, 1959 and trough deflectors January 17, 1963. *Salmon Trout* was supplied with four tenders: an LNER non-corridor; an LNER corridor; and two GNR 5,000 gal. Photograph courtesy of Colourrail.

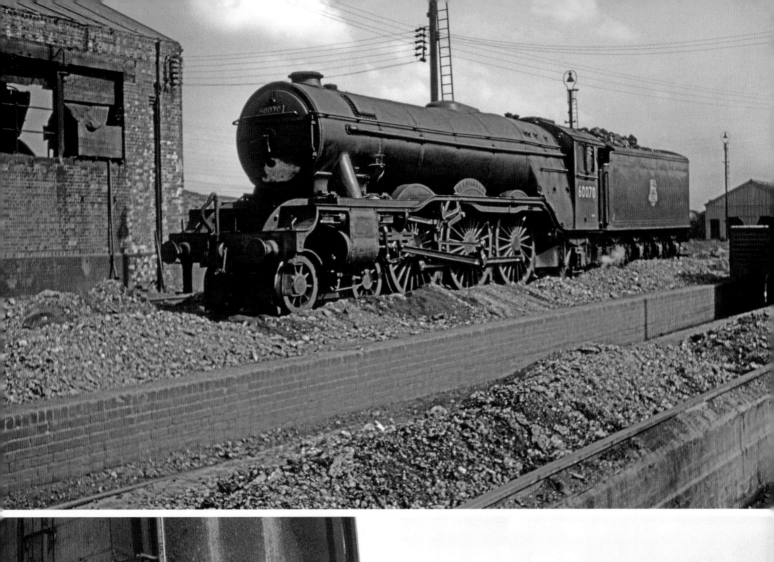

Above No. 60080 *Dick Turpin*

Initially, Doncaster shed was a 12-track through road shed with four slated hipped roofs. During the 1950s the facility was reduced to a 9-track through road building and the roof was clad with corrugated sheeting. No. 60080 *Dick Turpin* is at Doncaster Carr shed on November 12, 1955. Between October 20, 1955 and November 11, 1955, the engine had undergone a Light Casual repair at Doncaster Works. At this period the locomotive was allocated to Heaton. Photograph by Bill Reed.

Opposite above No. 60051 *Blink Bonny*

Muskham Water Troughs was one of six of its kind on the East Coast Main line and the third when travelling north on the route. The Muskham Troughs were 41 miles from Werrington Troughs to the south and 24 miles from Scrooby Water Troughs to the north. By 1924 LNER mechanical engineers had agreed that the setting on water troughs on the ECML should be standardised. As a result, the troughs extended two inches above rail level and the tender scoop dropped no more than one inch below rail level. Completed as an A1 during November 1924 at Doncaster Works, no. 60051 *Blink Bonny* was fitted with long travel valves by November 1927. Rebuilding to A3 was undertaken by November 1945. The engine is hurtling through Muskham Troughs on June 2, 1956. At this time the engine was allocated to Leeds Copley Hill. Photograph by Bill Reed.

Opposite below no. 60100 *Spearmint*

Doncaster Works Paint Shop was completed c. 1900 and contained eight roads with shallow pits. The roof was designed in a way to allow the north light to illuminate the interior. Paint storage was confined to the east end of the building which also housed machinery used in grinding and mixing colour. Photographer Bill Reed captured no. 60100 *Spearmint* in Doncaster Works Paint Shop during the 1950s.

Above **No. 60067** *Ladas*

In a view looking south west from York Road platform, no. 60067 *Ladas,* with a badly scorched smoke box, is leaving King's Cross heading a relief express to York and Hull on April 3, 1958. At the time of the photograph, *Ladas* was allocated to Doncaster. During its service life, the engine was paired with a GNR 5,000 gal. tender; an LNER corridor tender; and an LNER non-corridor tender. Photograph by Ben Brooksbank.

Opposite above **No. 60043** *Brown Jack*

No. 60043 *Brown Jack* is at Edinburgh Haymarket shed on September 18, 1955. St Margarets was Brown Jack's only other shed before withdrawal on May 14, 1964. During the 1890s it was decided by the NBR that a new locomotive shed at Edinburgh was required. The contract for constructing the new building – Edinburgh Haymarket – was given to Messrs James Young & Sons of Edinburgh for a price of £24,500 but due to delays only £13,719 was paid to the contractors. Photograph by Bill Reed.

Opposite below **No. 60042** *Singapore*

No. 60042 *Singapore* is on the Down line (ECML) with a northbound express picking up water at Muskham Water Troughs, just north of Newark. Doncaster Works built the engine as an A3 and it entered service on December 1, 1934. *Singapore* was attached to six tenders: three different GNR 5,000 gal; two LNER non-corridor; and one streamlined non-corridor. A double chimney was fitted from September 5, 1958 and trough deflectors, September 5, 1962. Withdrawal was from St Margarets on July 13, 1964. Photograph by Bill Reed.

Above **No. 60082 *Neil Gow***

The NBLC built no. 60082 *Neil Gow* and the locomotive entered service as an A1, no. 2581, during November 1924. Long travel valves were fitted from January 1929 and rebuilding to A3 completed by January 1943. The engine was initially allocated to Heaton and remained there until a switch to Gateshead in June 1948. *Neil Gow* was paired with three different GNR 5,000 gal. tenders during its existence. The photograph was taken at Chaloner's Whin, south of York, on May 26 1957 and is reproduced courtesy of Colourrail.

Opposite above **No. 60049 *Galtee More***

Heading an express on the Down line, between Bawtry and Rossington stations, no. 60049, *Galtee More* has just passed under a bridge carrying the Great North Road on July 14, 1957. Ten days later, the engine entered Doncaster Works for a Heavy Intermediate repair, re-emerging on September 17, 1957. Apart from a Light repair lasting only eight days during October 1924 at Gorton Works, *Galtee More* received maintenance at Doncaster Works throughout its entire working life. Photograph by Bill Reed.

Opposite below **No. 60099 *Call Boy***

Seen adjacent to Edinburgh Haymarket shed's general offices and turntable (out of view to the left) is no. 60099 *Call Boy* displaying 'The Queen of Scots' headboard on April 11, 1957. Entering service from Doncaster Works, as an A3, on April 19, 1930, the engine was allocated to Haymarket where it remained until January 12, 1940. A second allocation was made between October 19, 1940 and January 6, 1963. Photograph by Bill Reed.

Above **No. 60064** *Tagalie*

In a view facing south no. 60064 *Tagalie* is pulling away from Peterborough North with a Down express on August 16, 1958. Waiting to cross into New England Yard is an O2 2-8-0 on a Down empties. The ex-Midland lines are on the right. In the distance, beyond the station, is the Crescent Bridge. *Tagalie* was fitted with a double chimney in May, 1959 and was one of only a few A3s not fitted with trough deflectors. After withdrawal the locomotive was cut up at Doncaster during September 1961. Photograph by Ben Brooksbank.

Opposite above **No. 60104** *Solario*

No. 60104 *Solario* is at Marylebone station in the 1950s and about to depart with 'The Master Cutler'. Between June 4, 1954 and September 1, 1957, the engine had allocations at Leicester GC (twice) and Neasden. Only two tenders, both GNR type, were carried throughout its working life. A double chimney was fitted from April 24, 1959; *Solario* never carried trough deflectors. Withdrawal came from King's Cross on Monday December 7, 1959 and scrapping was carried out at Doncaster Works. The 'Master Cutler' train operated between Sheffield Victoria and London Marylebone, but after 1958 to London King's Cross. Photograph by Bill Reed.

Opposite below **No. 60082** *Neil Gow*

Maintenance on no. 60082 *Neil Gow* was undertaken at Gateshead Works, Darlington Works and Doncaster Works but exclusively at the latter from October 1950. A double chimney was fitted from September 18, 1959 and trough deflectors August 25, 1961. Withdrawal was from Gateshead on Monday September 2, 1963 and scrapping at Darlington Works during February 1964. Photograph of no. 60082 *Neil Gow* leaving York with Newcastle to Liverpool train by Eric Treacy, from the David Joy collection.

Above **No. 60075** *St Frusquin*

St Frusquin emerged from the NBLC, as an A1, no 2574, during October, 1924 with both vacuum and Westinghouse brakes (removed April. 1934). The initial allocation was to Gateshead, remaining there until August 1952. Darlington Works fitted long travel valves in December 1928 but rebuilding to A3 was completed at Doncaster Works by June 1942. Doncaster was also responsible for conversion from right hand to left hand drive, April 1954 and fitting a double chimney, August 1959. The engine was only paired with GNR tenders and four different ones were attached during its existence. Withdrawal was off Gateshead on Monday January 13, 1964; cutting up at Darlington Works. *St Frusquin* is at Marshall Meadows with a King's Cross - Glasgow train. Photograph by Eric Treacy from the David Joy collection.

Opposite **No. 60072** *Sunstar*

Built by the NBLC as an A1, no 2571 entered traffic with vacuum and Westinghouse brakes (removed in 1933) during September, 1924. The first allocation was to Gateshead, remaining there until March 1943. Darlington Works fitted long travel valves during a 94-day General repair completed in March, 1928. Until October 1931, *Sunstar* was maintained by Works at Darlington, Gateshead and Doncaster but afterwards entirely at the latter. Rebuilding to A3 was completed by July 1941. For five months, March to August, 1948, the engine carried the BR temporary number E72. *Sunstar* was only attached to two tenders: a GNR 5,000 gal. and an LNER non-corridor. The engine was supplied with four Diagram 94 boilers; one Diagram 94HP; and six Diagram 94A. Withdrawal was off Heaton on Monday October 22, 1962; scrapping undertaken at Doncaster from May 1963. Photograph of *Sunstar* leaving York with a Newcastle to Liverpool train on April 10, 1954 by Eric Treacy from the David Joy collection.

Above **60078 Night Hawk**

No. 60078 *Night Hawk* hurries through Holbeck, Leeds, during April 1958 with a passenger service bound for Liverpool. Completed by the NBLC as an A1, no. 2577, on October 24, 1924, the engine was initially equipped with both vacuum and Westinghouse brakes (removed by April, 1934). The first allocation was to Gateshead before a move to York on January 7, 1937. The engine was involved in a derailment in 1938. By January 1944, *Night Hawk* was rebuilt to A3 specifications; converted from right to left hand drive, August 28, 1953; fitted with a double chimney, February 27, 1959; and trough deflectors were added in March 1962. Photograph *Yorkshire Post Newspapers*.

Below No. 60058 *Blair Athol*

No. 60058 *Blair Athol* enters Leeds City station from the east on the former Leeds-Selby main line with the 14.30 from Newcastle on June 10, 1959. Entering service as an A1, no 2557, from Doncaster Works on February 28, 1925, the first allocation, for a brief period, was to Gorton. Thereafter, a long stint of over 17 years was to Grantham. Rebuilding to A3 was carried out by December 8, 1945; conversion from right hand to left hand drive, March 30, 1953; and a double chimney fitted by October 3, 1958. During its lifetime the engine had no fewer than nine tenders, eight GNR 5,000 gal. and one streamlined non-corridor. Withdrawal from Heaton was affected in June 1963; scrapping was undertaken at Doncaster Works. Photograph by Ben Brooksbank.

Above **No. 60061** *Pretty Polly*

No. 60061 *Pretty Polly* is pulling away from Newcastle during June 1959 at the head of Anglo-Scottish Car Carrier. The service between King's Cross and Perth began in 1955 and transported both passengers and motorcars until withdrawn in 1988. No. 60061 was adjusted to 75% cut-off by April, 1947; double chimney and trough deflectors fitted, October, 1958 and February, 1962. *Pretty Polly* was paired with five different GNR 5,000 gal. tenders during its existence and withdrawal off Grantham was affected during September 1963; scrapping was at Doncaster. Photograph reproduced courtesy of Colourrail'.

Opposite above and below **No. 60035** *Windsor Lad*

Erected as an A3 at Doncaster Works and entering service on July 10, 1934, as no. 2500 *Windsor Lad* (later nos 570, 35 and finally 60035), the engine was allocated to Haymarket. Apart from a short period at Aberdeen Ferryhill, in 1937, *Windsor Lad* remained at Haymarket until April 23, 1961 when a four month stay at Carlisle Canal began. Apart from two Light repairs at Cowlairs in 1941 and a Light Casual at Darlington,1958, Doncaster Works undertook all work on the locomotive. This included adjustment to 75% cut-off by October, 1955; and fitting double chimney, January 1959. *Windsor Lad* was attached to only one (LNER non-corridor) tender throughout its working life. It was supplied with eight different boilers – six Diagram 94A and two Diagram 94HP.

In the bottom photograph no. 60035 is heading a service from Hawick station to Carlise. The station was opened by the North British Railway on October 29, 1849 but was resited slightly to the south for the completion of the second phase of the Waverley line between Hawick and Carlisle. Closure came on January 6, 1969, though the site was not cleared until January 1975. Both pictures by Bill Reed.

No. 60106 *Flying Fox*

This location at Grantham station looking over to platform 1 was seemingly a favourite with railway photographers and Bill Reed may be counted amongst them, capturing a number of locomotives, particularly A3s from this vantage point. The station was opened in 1852 on the GNR line from Peterborough to Retford. No. 60106 *Flying Fox* was rebuilt to A3 during a 47 day Heavy repair at Doncaster Works between January 28, 1947 and March 15, 1947. The engine received its Brunswick Green livery after a General repair was completed on April 20, 1952.

No. 60041 *Salmon Trout*

During the 1930s a shed in existence at Perth since the late 1850s was considered inadequate by the LMS, and an improvement scheme was embarked upon. Another shed was built directly to the south of the old building, with the new structure containing eight through roads and a two track repair shop adjoined the west side. BR closed the site in May 1967 and the area was redeveloped to include housing, a supermarket and an industrial estate. Pictured at Perth shed, no 60041 *Salmon Trout* was withdrawn from St Margarets on December 4, 1965. Scrapping was carried out at Arnott Young's, Carmyle during September 1966. Photograph by Bill Reed.

No. 60038 *Firdaussi*

No. 60038 *Firdaussi* is on the Edinburgh Haymarket shed turntable – 70 feet in length – and built by Ransomes & Rapier. Installed around 1931, it was originally manually operated but fitted with a vacuum motor after WWII. Built at Doncaster Works, *Firdaussi* went to traffic as an A3 from August 11, 1934 and spent much of its time allocated to sheds in the North East, but during the early 1960s was at Holbeck and Neville Hill. A double chimney was fitted at Doncaster from September 30, 1959. Two LNER non-corridor tenders were carried through its working existence which came to an end on Monday November 18, 1963. Photograph by Bill Reed.

Above No. **60046** *Diamond Jubilee*

No. 60046 *Diamond Jubilee* is at the northern end of Doncaster shed with a Thompson B1 Class 4-6-0 and D16/3 4-4-0 no. 62599 for company. Entering service as an A1 from Doncaster Works on August 9, 1924, the engine was allocated to Gorton. Rebuilding to A3 was completed at Doncaster by August 23, 1941. Withdrawal from Grantham occurred on Sunday June 16, 1963. Photograph by Bill Reed.

Below No. **60055** *Woolwinder*

No. 60055 *Woolwinder* is at Gateshead on March 23, 1960. Apart from a Light repair at Gorton Works in 1939, the engine was always maintained at Doncaster Works and was cut up there during September 1961. Photograph courtesy of Colourrail.

No. 60036 *Colombo*

To the rear in this photograph, Darlington shed was built by the LNER in 1940 and comprised several roads open at both ends. This replaced an earlier facility located on the same site, which was established by the NER in 1885. No. 60036 *Colombo* was completed as an A3 at Doncaster Works in July 1934 and allocated to Gateshead. The engine underwent a Light repair March/April, 1947 at Doncaster Works following a collision at Peterborough. Adjustment to 75% cut-off was undertaken by April 1956. The double chimney was fitted between August 29, 1958 and November 14, 1958 when the locomotive was at Doncaster Works undergoing a General repair and other work following a buffer stop collision at York. Trough deflectors were fitted from July 19, 1962. *Colombo* arrived at Darlington shed on December 15, 1963 after previous stints at York (North), Heaton, King's Cross, Neville Hill, Copley Hill, and Ardsley. Photograph by Bill Reed.

No. 60043 *Brown Jack*

Haymarket's facilities included a water tank, turntable and a ramped coal stage, eventually replaced by a mechanical coaler. The shed closed to steam on September 9, 1963 and a new diesel depot was erected on the site. On entering service from Doncaster Works on February 9, 1935, no. 60043 *Brown Jack* was the last A3 to be built. Photographed at the south side of Edinburgh Haymarket shed the engine is shown with a double chimney, fitted from February 21, 1959. The engine was sold for scrap to Motherwell, Machinery & Scrap Co, Wishaw in July, 1964. Photograph by Bill Reed.

No. 60048 *Doncaster*

Several sheds were in existence before a new brick-built four-track dead-ended facility – was constructed at Grantham in 1897. Comprising a ramped coal stage and a turntable the latter was replaced in 1947 by a turning triangle. Re-roofed in 1955, the shed was closed on September 9, 1963. No. 60048 *Doncaster* is at Grantham with the mechanical coaling plant – in the distance to the right . This was erected early in 1937 by Henry Lees & Co. Ltd for approx. £5,600. The engine was allocated to Grantham when new and would return there a further three times during its service life. Photograph by Bill Reed.

Above No. **60066** *Merry Hampton*
Entering service as an A1, from the NBLC, on July 16, 1924, *Merry Hampton* was allocated to Edinburgh Haymarket, and in May 1926, the engine was involved in a derailment at Cramlington, nine miles from Newcastle. Thankfully, this did not result in any serious injuries but the locomotive underwent repairs at Darlington Works between June 8, 1926 and September 15, 1926. Rebuilding to A3 was completed at Doncaster Works by December 9, 1945. *Merry Hampton* is at Grantham station's platform 1. Photograph by Bill Reed.

Below No. **60056** *Centenary*
Rushing through Great Ponton, Grantham, with an express, is no. 60056 *Centenary,* pictured just after the fitting of double chimney, July 1959 and before receiving trough deflectors, August, 1961. Photograph by Bill Reed.

No. 60061 *Pretty Polly*

No. 60061 *Pretty Polly* pauses at Grantham's platform 1. A double chimney was fitted in October 1958 and *Pretty Polly* is seen with small wing deflectors near the chimney to help disperse the exhaust. The engine was one of four A3s to have this type of deflector fitted in November 1959. Larger trough deflectors were fixed by February 3, 1962. Withdrawal was from Grantham on Sunday September 8, 1963 after over 38 years service. Photograph by Bill Reed.

Above No. 60055 *Woolwinder*

The distance between Retford station (in North Nottinghamshire) and King's Cross is approx. 138½ miles. On the southern approach to the station the line falls at a gradient of 1 in 178 before becoming level. North of the station the line rises at 1 in 440 for a short distance before falling at 1 in 198 and then becoming level. Running on the ECML at Retford with an express during the last period of its existence is no. 60055 *Woolwinder*, named after the 1907 Doncaster St Leger horse race winner owned by Col. E.W. Baird. From having a double chimney fitted during June, 1958, the engine worked just over an additional three years. During that short time, Doncaster Works was visited three times for a General (with a boiler change) and two Light Casual repairs. This amounted to a total of 86 days out of service. Photograph by Bill Reed.

Above No. 60064 *Tagalie*

From a similar spot shown earlier in the book, photographer Bill Reed is once more facing south and looking towards a road bridge carrying the Great North Road, between Bawtry and Rossington, South Yorkshire. This time he has captured no. 60064 *Tagalie* hurrying past on the down line with an express. The ECML rises at a gradient of 1:198 approaching Bawtry before it falls at a gradient of 1:198 between Bawtry and Doncaster. The line becomes level again between Rossington and Doncaster. Repairs on the locomotive were shared between Cowlairs Works and Doncaster Works until 1945. Thereafter, it was Doncaster Works only. *Tagalie* was another A3 not fitted with trough deflectors.

Opposite No. 60068 *Sir Visto*

Displaying 'The Waverley' passenger service headboard, no. 60068 *Sir Visto* is ready to head the train from Carlisle to Edinburgh. Pictured at Carlisle Canal shed, the engine was one of a number of the class on hand there for the service. Beginning in 1927 as the 'Thames-Forth Express', departing from London St Pancras and destined for Edinburgh Waverley station, the service ceased in 1968. To service as an A1 from the NBLC during August 1924, *Sir Visto* was the last of the A1s (at the time classified A10) to be rebuilt to A3 in December 1948. Arriving at Carlisle Canal shed from Eastfield on November 20, 1940, the engine stayed there until withdrawal. Between 1924 and 1943 *Sir Visto* was maintained at Cowlairs Works and Doncaster Works but afterwards entirely at the latter. During service, the engine carried two GNR type tenders and one streamlined non-corridor tender. A double chimney was fitted in April 1959 though no large trough deflectors were ever fixed. Photograph by Bill Reed.

No. 60071 *Tranquil*

No. 60071 *Tranquil* is located beside offices at Haymarket shed after being fitted with a double chimney by July 4, 1958. Before withdrawal the engine would visit Doncaster Works five more times. The work including; a Light Casual; General, with a change of boiler; General, with a change of boiler; a Heavy Casual; and a Light Casual. Photograph by Bill Reed.

Above No. 60078 *Night Hawk*

No. 60078 *Night Hawk* is at Edinburgh Haymarket shed and throughout its existence was attached to only two GNR 5,000 gal. tenders. The engine's repairs were carried out in the Works at Gateshead, Darlington and Doncaster. Withdrawal was from Heaton on October 22, 1962 and cutting up carried out at Doncaster Works in May, 1963. Photograph by Bill Reed.

Above **No. 60080** *Dick Turpin*

Contrary to general practice on naming the A3s, *Dick Turpin* was never the name of a winning race horse. Seemingly, the infamy surrounding the character was deemed appropriate for the name of a locomotive. Under a General repair, lasting from the end of 1928 until January 1929, Darlington Works fitted long travel valves to the engine. Doncaster Works removed *Dick Turpin*'s Westinghouse pump 1934; undertook rebuilding the engine to A3, 1942; and made the 75% cut off adjustment, 1946. A double chimney and trough deflectors were fitted at Doncaster Works between October, 1959 and November, 1961. *Dick Turpin* was attached to five different GNR 5,000 gal. tenders during its working life. Allocations from 1924 to 1960 were in the North East but a move to the Leeds area sheds Holbeck, Ardsley and Neville Hill, occurred 1960 to 1963 where the locomotive could be seen sometimes fronting the 'Thames-Clyde Express'. There was a return to Gateshead shed from December 8, 1963 until withdrawal from there on October 12, 1964. Scrapping was undertaken by A. Draper, Hull, two months later. Photograph taken at Doncaster shed by Bill Reed.

Opposite above and below **No. 60073** *St Gatien*

The top picture illustrates no. 60073 *St Gatien* standing on the east side of Edinburgh Haymarket shed and waiting to join the Edinburgh & Glasgow railway line. The line was opened during February 1842. The picture below shows the same locomotive next to the turntable pit on no. 2 road at the east end of the shed. Completed by the NBLC as LNER no. 2572, during October 1924, *St Gatien* was initially fitted with both vacuum and Westinghouse brakes, the latter being removed during February 1933. Until October 1936 the engine was maintained at Darlington Works (General repairs), Gateshead Works (Light repairs) and Doncaster Works (General repairs) but thereafter at the latter Works only. Long travel valves were fitted at Darlington Works by December, 1927. Rebuilding to A3 was completed at Doncaster Works by November 1945; adjustment to 75% cut off, November 1953; a double chimney and trough deflectors fitted by August 1958 and July 1961 respectively. Apart from a three year allocation to York between 1943 and 1946 *St Gatien* was always allocated to sheds in the North East. Withdrawal from Gateshead occurred on Monday August 19, 1963. Both photographs by Bill Reed.

Above No. **60084** *Trigo*

No. 60084 *Trigo* is beside the water tower at Leeds Neville Hill shed c. 1960. Entering service as LNER A3 no. 2595 from Doncaster Works on February 22, 1930, the engine was allocated to Gateshead staying there for over 13 years. Following nearly a three year stint at Heaton, *Trigo* returned to Gateshead. A move to Neville Hill, Leeds followed, extending from September 1949 to December 8, 1963. Another allocation to Gateshead lasted until withdrawal on November 23, 1964. Doncaster Works was responsible for maintenance to the locomotive throughout its service existence: modification to 75% cut-off was carried out during December 1947; a double chimney fitted by July 1958; and trough deflectors January 1962. Until November 28, 1940 the engine was attached to an LNER non-corridor tender; afterwards a streamlined non-corridor tender, as seen here. Photograph by Bill Reed.

Opposite No. **60079** *Bayardo*

No. 60079 *Bayardo* is at the east side of Edinburgh Haymarket shed. As LNER no. 2578, the engine was one of 20 A1s to be erected by the NBLC between August and December 1924. *Bayardo* entered service in October 1924 and was named at Gateshead Works at the end of October, 1925. From the outset, the engine was equipped with both vacuum and Westinghouse brakes and was amongst the first five A1s to be rebuilt to A3 specifications. The conversion work on *Bayardo* was undertaken at Darlington Works and completed in May 1928. Long travel valves were also fitted at this time. A double chimney was installed by January 1960 but *Bayardo* never had trough deflectors. When the photograph was taken c. 1960, *Bayardo* was allocated to Carlisle Canal shed, extending from May 30, 1948 until withdrawal on September 11, 1961. Photograph by Bill Reed.

Above **No. 60089** *Felstead*

No. 60089 *Felstead* is at Edinburgh St Margarets shed (the second of three) which opened in 1866. It was a six track dead-ended facility with a slated twin-gable style roof. Closure by BR was affected on May 1, 1967 and the area was subsequently cleared. Apart from an Unclassified attention at St Rollox Works in 1961, the engine was maintained at Doncaster Works throughout its service existence. Photograph by Bill Reed.

Opposite **No. 60088** *Book Law*

No. 60088 *Book Law* is at Grantham with the shed's mechanical coaler (west of Grantham station) to the right. Entering service as A3 no. 2599 from Doncaster Works during July 1930, the engine was allocated to Gateshead, staying there until 1937. A further three stints would be served there until withdrawal during October, 1963. All *Book Law*'s maintenance, apart from a brief visit to Gateshead Works in March 1954, was undertaken at Doncaster Works. The modification to 75% cut off was carried out during August 1957 and a double chimney fitted by February 1959. The engine was supplied with five tenders: two LNER non-corridor and three GNR type. *Book Law* went into Darlington Works for cutting up during November 1963. Photograph by Bill Reed.

Above No. 60090 *Grand Parade*

No. 60090 *Grand Parade* is standing adjacent to the Weigh House at Doncaster Works. Known as The Plant, Doncaster Works was established in 1853 by the Great Northern Railway Company and in subsequent years was greatly expanded to include a Paint Shop, New Erecting shop, and locomotive and tender repair shops (known as the Crimpsall Repair Shops). From July 1950 until withdrawal in October 1963, *Grand Parade* was allocated to Scottish sheds. During its working life the locomotive was attached to three LNER corridor tenders and seven GNR 5,000 gal. tenders. All the maintenance work was carried out at Doncaster Works and the engine is pictured with a double chimney fitted from August 1958; trough deflectors were added in January 1963. Following withdrawal from St Rollox, *Grand Parade* was cut up at Cowlairs. In 1987 Doncaster Works was split up into three separate businesses – only two presently survive. Photograph by Bill Reed.

Opposite above and below No. 60093 *Coronach*

In the top picture, no 60093 *Coronach* is seen at Carlisle Canal shed; in the one below at Carlisle Citadel station. Named after the winner of the 1926 Derby and St. Leger, the engine was built as an A3, LNER no. 2747, and entered traffic from Doncaster Works on November 24, 1928. The first allocation was to Doncaster shed until March 1930 and a transfer to King's Cross. A return to Doncaster occurred after two months and *Coronach* was stabled there for just under nine years. A move from Haymarket to Carlisle Canal began on January 23, 1941 and ended when the engine was withdrawn in April 1962. Both photographs by Bill Reed.

No. 60100 Spearmint
No. 60100 *Spearmint* is at Edinburgh Haymarket shed with a double chimney that was fitted during July 1959 at Doncaster Works, where all its maintenance was carried out. In subsequent years the smoke-box door would have the lamp iron bracket and number plate lowered and the handrail rail split into two. Trough deflectors were added in June, 1961. Photograph by Bill Reed.

Above **No. 60097** *Humorist*

No. 60097 *Humorist* is entering Perth South shed from the north end; the bridge in the distance carries Edinburgh Road. The brick-built eight track through road shed was opened during May 1938 and included a 70ft turntable, repair shop, mechanical coaler, and water tank. Closure to steam occurred on May 14, 1967, to all traffic October 5, 1969. Three years later the building was demolished. *Humorist* was allocated to Doncaster, Grantham and King's Cross before arriving in the Scottish region at Haymarket in July 1950. Apart from a month in 1954, when allocated to Carlisle Canal shed, the engine was at Haymarket until December 1961. Humorist was only paired with two 5,000 gal. tenders throughout its existence and was supplied with a number of boilers: four Diagram 94HP; seven Diagram 94A; and one Diagram 107. St Margarets was *Humorist's* last allocation before withdrawal in August 1963. Photograph by Bill Reed.

Above No. **60098** *Spion Kop*

Pictured at Edinburgh Haymarket shed, with a section of the Murrayfield stadium visible to the rear on the left, no. 60098 *Spion Kop*, was the last member of the first order of A3s to be completed. Entering service from Doncaster Works in April 1929, the first allocation was to Doncaster, lasting just under nine years, before a very brief sojourn at Haymarket and St Margarets in 1938. A return to Haymarket in August 1950 lasted until January 1963 and a move to St Margarets occurred, this being the last shed before withdrawal in October 1963. From October 1956, the engine carried three Diagram 94A boilers and the banjo dome is visible here. Adjustment to 75% cut off was also completed by October 1956. Photograph by Bill Reed.

Opposite above and below No **60101** *Cicero*

Both views show No 60101 *Cicero* at Edinburgh Haymarket shed. Built as an A3 and entering service from Doncaster Works on June 4, 1930, the engine spent its entire working life allocated to Scottish sheds. Only two LNER non-corridor tenders were supplied throughout the A3's existence. Adjustment to 75% cut off was carried out in January 1957; a double chimney fitted from July 1958 followed by trough deflectors in July 1961. Apart from a three-day Light repair at Cowlairs Works during October 1942 all the engine's maintenance was carried out at Doncaster Works. Withdrawal from St Margarets occurred on April 11, 1963. Scrapping was at Arnott Young, Carmyle during June 1964. In the bottom picture *Cicero* is carrying 'The Heart of Midlothian' headboard; the service ran between King's Cross - Edinburgh Waverley, from 1951 to 1968. Both photographs by Bill Reed.

No. 60107 *Royal Lancer*

Situated just north of Doncaster shed is no. 60107 *Royal Lancer*. A double chimney was fitted in 1959 and trough deflectors, 1962. The engine is attached to a GNR 5,000 gallon tender, carried from February, 1943 until withdrawal. Doncaster Works carried out all the engine's maintenance though it was never allocated to the town's shed. Photograph by Bill Reed.

Above and below No. 60107 *Royal Lancer*
Two further photographs of no. 60107 *Royal Lan*cer show the locomotive at Grantham(above) and Retford (below). Withdrawal was off Grantham on Sunday September 1, 1963 and cutting up carried out at Doncaster Works. Both photographs by Bill Reed.

No. 60106 *Flying Fox*

No. 60106 *Flying Fox* is at Grantham shed. The engine was fitted with three Diagram 94A boilers between December 1953 until withdrawal. Conversion from right to left hand drive was completed by December 1953; a double chimney and trough deflectors were fitted from November 1958 and October 1961 respectively. The engine was allocated four times to Grantham shed. Withdrawal was from New England in December 1964 and scrapping carried out by R.A. King, Norwich during 1965. Photograph by Bill Reed.

Above No. 60102 *Sir Frederick Banbury*

In a view facing north east, no. 60102 *Sir Frederick Banbury* pulls away from York past the Racecourse platforms. Converting the locomotive from right to left hand drive was completed by March 1953; adjustment to 75% cut-off, December 1956; and fitting a double chimney, April, 1959. Withdrawal was off King's Cross during November 1961 and cutting up at Doncaster Works. Photograph by Bill Reed.

Below No. 60108 *Gay Crusader*

No. 60108 *Gay Crusader* entered service from Doncaster Works as an A1 during June 1923 and was allocated to the town's shed until a move to Grantham in November 1934. The engine would return to Doncaster shed another four times and was pictured there by Bill Reed.

No. 60111 Enterprise

Looking in a south easterly direction, no. 60111 *Enterprise* is visible on the west side of Grantham shed. Immediately to the rear and on the right is the water softener, and beyond the old coaling stage and mechanical coaler. *Enterprise* entered traffic from Doncaster Works as A1 no. 1480 on August 17, 1923. Rebuilding to A3 was completed during July 1927 along with the addition of long travel valves. The engine was first allocated to Grantham and would return there a further three times. Doncaster Works carried out other alterations to the locomotive including: conversion from right to left hand drive (January–March 1953); increase to 75% cut off (February–April 1956); fitting double chimney (May–June 1959); and adding trough deflectors (March–April 1962). Withdrawal was from Grantham during December 1962 and cutting up at Doncaster early in the following year. Photograph by Bill Reed.

Above No. **60089** *Felstead*
Adjustment to 75% cut off was carried out on no. 60089 *Felstead*, seen here at Edinburgh Haymarket shed, by February 1955. A double chimney and trough deflectors were fitted by October 1959 and November 1961 respectively. Photograph by Bill Reed.

Below No. **60112** *St Simon*
Rushing towards Retford, no. 60112 *St Simon* was withdrawn from New England, December 1964. Photograph by Bill Reed.

No. 60095 *Flamingo*

No. 60095 *Flamingo* entered service as an A3, no 2749, from Doncaster Works on January 26, 1929 and was allocated to the town's shed. Staying there for just 11 days, the engine moved to Carlisle Canal and was there until withdrawal. *Flamingo* was renumbered 558 (LNER 1946 1st), March 1946; 95 (LNER 1946 2nd), May 1946; 60095 (BR September 1948). The streamlined non-corridor tender, seen here, was attached to the locomotive from February 1954. Prior to this time the engine was supplied with three GNR 5,000 gal. tenders and one LNER corridor tender. Withdrawal was from Carlisle Canal in April 1961 and the engine returned to Doncaster Works to be cut up. Photograph taken at Edinburgh Haymarket by Bill Reed.

Above No. 60036 *Colombo*

No. 60036 *Colombo* was photographed at Darlington shed near the turntable on October 3, 1964 . On the apparatus is the preserved no. 4472 *Flying Scotsman*, which had worked 'The Darlington Marquess' railtour north from King's Cross to Harrogate. There, the also preserved, K4 no. 3442 *The Great Marquess* piloted the train to Darlington. *Colombo* was condemned at Darlington on Monday, November 23, 1964; scrapping carried out at A. Draper, Hull during January 1965. Photograph by Bill Reed.

Below No. 60065 *Knight of Thistle*

No. 60065 *Knight of Thistle* – recently a recipient of the smoke deflectors – is stood alongside Deltic D9018 *Ballymoss* at Doncaster Works during November 1961. The diesel had just arrived from Vulcan Foundry for acceptance before ousting A3s on the expresses. Withdrawal for the A3 was from New England during June, 1964. Photograph by Ben Burrell.

Above and opposite **No. 60045** *Lemberg*

Two views taken on October 3, 1964 show no. *60045 Lemberg* inside Darlington shed. The facility opened in 1940, and comprised a low multi-pitched rood and seven through roads. There was a mechanical coaling plant, a two track repair shed and a 70ft turntable. The shed replaced one of 60ft dating from 1906. Closure by British Rail occurred on March 27, 1966 and the site was cleared.

Named after the winner of the 1910 Derby, no. 60045 *Lemberg* was largely allocated to North Eastern sheds – six times at Darlington. Throughout its service life, the engine was only attached to two GNR 5,000 gal. tenders. Apart from a Light Casual at Darlington Works December 1949/January 1950 all the maintenance was undertaken at Doncaster Works. Conversion from right hand to left hand drive was completed by October 1953; adjustment to 75% cut off, January 1958; double chimney and trough deflectors fitted, October 1959 and November 1962 respectively. *Lemberg* worked with five different Diagram 94A boilers from February 1949 until withdrawal off Darlington shed occurred, Monday November 23, 1964. Scrapping was by A. Draper, Hull, January 1965. Both photographs by Bill Reed.

Above No. **60089** *Felstead*

From February, 1951 to November 1960 no. 60089 *Felstead* was allocated to Edinburgh Haymarket shed; then Dundee Tay Bridge until December 1960. The engine is seen above at Dundee Tay Bridge in May 1961 whilst allocated to St Margarets. This was *Felstead*'s last shed before withdrawal in October 1963. Cutting up was completed at Inverurie by February 1964. Photograph by Bill Reed.

Opposite top No. **60047** *Donovan*

No. 60047 *Donovan* is passing through Great Ponton, south of Grantham, during May 1961. The engine was attached to five different GNR 5,000 gal. tenders during its time in traffic. It was also supplied with the following boilers: four Diagram 94; four Diagram 94A; and one Diagram 94HP. Photograph by Bill Reed.

Opposite below No. **60049** *Galtee More*

No. 60049 *Galtee More* glides through Great Ponton during May 1961. A double chimney was fitted to the engine from March 4, 1959 and trough deflectors, October 21, 1960. Withdrawal was off Grantham during December, 1962. Photograph by Bill Reed.

Above **No. 60099** *Call Boy*

No. 60099 *Call Boy* hauls a rake of carriages out of Edinburgh Waverley during July 1959. Doncaster Works carried out several modifications, including: adjustment to 75% cut off, by November 1956; fitting double chimney by August 1958 and trough deflectors, February 1962. *Call Boy* had two LNER non-corridor tenders; one LNER corridor; and one GNR 5,000 gal. Also fitted were three Diagram 94HP boilers; four Diagram 94A boilers; and three Diagram 107 boilers. During its existence, the engine was only allocated to two sheds: Haymarket and St Margarets. Withdrawal from the latter occurred on October 28, 1963. *Call Boy* was broken up at Arnott Young's, Carmyle in June of the following year. Photograph courtesy of Colourrail.

Opposite **No. 60059** *Tracery*

No. 60059 *Tracery* accelerates through Great Ponton during May 1961. Entering service, as A1 no. 2558, from Doncaster Works during March 1925, the engine was allocated for just under a month to Gorton. Thereafter, a move to Grantham lasted until September 1938 and a return to Gorton was noted until December 1942. Rebuilding to A3 was completed by July 1942. Photograph by Bill Reed.

Above **No. 60067** *Ladas*

On October 15, 1962, no. 60067 *Ladas* is at King's Cross shed, situated north of King's Cross station. The 40 acres of land on which the shed was created was bought from St Bartholomew's hospital for £40,000. In 1849 Lewis Cubitt prepared designs for the shed and some alterations were made by Edward Bury. The buildings were fully completed between 1851-52. The facility closed during June 1963 and the site cleared. *Ladas* was maintained at Gateshead Works, Cowlairs Works, Darlington Works and Doncaster Works. The latter Works was responsible for *Ladas*'s adjustment to 75% cut off by February 1950; conversion from right hand to left hand drive, August 1953; and fitting double chimney, April, 1959 and trough deflectors, July 1961. The engine had four Diagram 94HP boilers; two Diagram 94A boilers; and latterly one Diagram 107 boiler. Withdrawal from King's Cross occurred on Saturday December 29, 1962 and cutting up was carried out at Doncaster Works in January of the following year. Photograph by Bill Reed.

Above **No. 60076** *Galopin*

No. 60076 *Galopin* is at Darlington station with an express parcels train on June 13, 1962. Improvements to the station which included an impressive three-span overall roof were completed during July 1887. Entering service as an A1 from the NBLC during October 1924, no. 2575 was fitted with both vacuum and Westinghouse brakes. The locomotive was initially allocated to Gateshead, remaining there until December 1948. Maintenance of the engine was carried out at Darlington Works, Gateshead Works and Doncaster Works (exclusively at the latter from March 1936 – apart from two Light Casuals at Darlington in 1949). Long travel valves were fitted from June 1928; the Westinghouse pump was removed May, 1934; rebuilding to A3 completed June 1941; right hand to left hand drive, by April 1954; and double chimney fitted by June, 1959. *Galopin* was attached to four different GNR type tenders and worked with six Diagram 94 boilers; and five Diagram 94A boilers. Throughout its existence, the engine alternated between Gateshead and Darlington sheds but for nearly two months before withdrawal on October 29, 1962 was at Heaton. Scrapping was at Doncaster Works from April 1963. Photograph by Bill Reed.

Above No. 60110 *Robert the Devil*

No. 60110 *Robert the Devil* has some young admirers at Newcastle Central station. The engine was consistently maintained at Doncaster Works: adjustment to 75% cut off by March 1949; right hand to left hand drive, January 1953; double chimney fitted, May 1959 ; and trough deflectors, July 1961. *Robert the Devil* was the only A1/A3 to retain the same tender – a GNR 5,000 gal. – throughout its service life. Withdrawal was off King's Cross during May 1963. Photograph taken by Jack Teasdale and reproduced courtesy of Stephen Veitch.

Opposite No. 60062 *Minoru*

The driver and fireman of no. 60062 *Minoru* are seemingly taking a break to admire the view at Darlington on October 3, 1964. Completed, as A1 no. 2561, at Doncaster Works during May 1925, the initial allocation, lasting under a month, was to Gorton. Maintenance was carried out exclusively at Doncaster Works: long travel valves were fitted by November 1929; conversion to A3, June 1944; right hand to left hand drive, October 1952; double chimney fitted, February 1959; and trough deflectors, July 1961. *Minoru* was attached to four different GNR 5,000 gal. tenders; two streamlined non-corridor tenders; and two LNER non-corridor tenders. The engine had 15 boiler changes during its lifetime which ended at New England on Saturday December 26 1964. It was sold to R.A. King, Norwich for scrap during February 1965. Photograph by Bill Reed.

Above **No. 60059** *Tracery*
Viewed from Peterborough's Crescent Bridge, no. 60059 *Tracery* is approaching the city's station whilst working the Down 13.40 King's Cross - Leeds/Bradford express. Conversion of the locomotive from right hand to left hand drive was done by July 1954; adjustment to 75% cut off, April 1956; a double chimney and trough deflectors fitted, July 1958 and September respectively. *Tracery* was noted as being attached to three GNR 5,000 gal. tenders; one streamlined non-corridor tender; and fitted with seven Diagram 94 boilers; two Diagram 94HP and seven Diagram 94A. Withdrawal off King's Cross was implemented during December 1962 and cutting up carried out at Doncaster Works. Photograph by Ben Brooksbank.

Opposite **No. 60063** *Isinglass*
Peterborough New England shed was established by 1852 and could accommodate up to 24 engines. Three years later, two further lines were added to increase capacity. Further extensions took place in 1866 to provide the shed with nine lines which is how it remained until closure in 1968. No. 60063 *Isinglass* was pictured on December 8, 1963 on the east side of the New England shed, with the fitting and wagon repair shops on the right. Doncaster Works maintained the locomotive solely from September 1926, the work including: rebuilding to A3 by April 1946; conversion from right hand to left hand drive, November 1952; adjustment to 75% cut off August 1957; fitting double chimney and trough deflectors February 1959 and August 1961 respectively. *Isinglass* was attached to four different GNR 5,000 gal. tenders during its working life which came to a close at New England during June 1964. Scrapping was by R.A. King of Norwich during August 1964. Photograph by Bill Reed.

Above **No. 60052** *Prince Palatine*

Entering service from Doncaster Works as A1 no. 2551, during November 1924, the engine was allocated for just under three months to Gorton. A move to Grantham was to follow lasting until September 1943. Rebuilt to A3 by March 1940, *Prince Palatine* carried three more numbers: LNER (1946 1st) 520; LNER (1946 2nd) 52; and BR 60052. Adjustment to 75% cut off was in hand by November 1958; a double chimney fitted, November 1958; and trough deflectors, October 1962. Photograph of *Prince Palatine* at Newcastle reproduced courtesy of Colourrail.

Below **No. 60096** *Papyrus*

WD 2-8-0 locomotive no. 90444 and A3 4-6-2 no. 60096 *Papyrus* are depicted at Dundee Tay Bridge shed. The facility was located to the west of Dundee Tay Bridge and installed by the North British Railway during the 1890s. Comprising six through roads, the shed had its roof replaced during the late 1950s and early 1960s. Closure came in May 1967 and the shed had been demolished by the end of the decade. No. 2750, *Papyrus* was initially allocated to King's Cross remaining there until a move to Haymarket in August 1937. In 1935 the engine briefly held the speed record for steam traction at 108mph before A4 no. 2509 *Silver Link* pushed this to 112mph. *Papyrus* recorded another two periods at King's Cross but the engine was condemned at St Margarets during September, 1963. Photograph of *Papyrus* at Dundee Tay Bridge shed reproduced courtesy of Colourrail.

Above **No. 60109** *Hermit*

Doncaster Works fitted long travel valves to no. 60109 *Hermit* during April 1930 and continued to be responsible for the engine's maintenance. Rebuilding to A3 was undertaken by November, 1943; the LNER 1946 1st number, 508, applied from January, 1946; the LNER 1946 2nd number, 109, added from June 1946; adjustment to 75% cut-off March 1947; and BR number, 60109, applied from May 1948. Amongst the engine's allocations were five at Doncaster and four at King's Cross. *Hermit* was only attached to GNR 5,000 gal. tenders and five were noted during its history. It was also supplied with 12 different boilers. A double chimney was fitted by March 1959 and trough deflectors, January 1961. Photograph of *Hermit* at Eaton Wood supplied by Colourrail.

Opposite **No. 60066** *Merry Hampton*

Merry Hampton was a much travelled engine, having 23 allocations noted during its time in traffic and they were quite spread out over the country, including stints at Aberdeen Ferryhill, Carlisle Canal and King's Cross. For just under four months in 1929, the engine was attached to an LNER corridor tender, but before that and afterwards was noted with six different GNR type tenders. Cowlairs Works and Darlington Works were involved with maintenance work on the engine until 1938, thereafter it was Doncaster Works alone – apart from a Light repair at Cowlairs Works in February, 1948. Conversion from right to left hand drive was completed by January, 1953; adjustment to 75% cut-off, May 1957; a double chimney fitted October, 1958; and trough deflectors, October 1961. *Merry Hampton* had five allocations to King's Cross starting from October 1950 and is seen at the shed in a photograph reproduced courtesy of Colourrail. Withdrawal from Grantham occurred on Sunday September 8, 1963 after just over 39 years' service. Cutting up was at Doncaster Works.

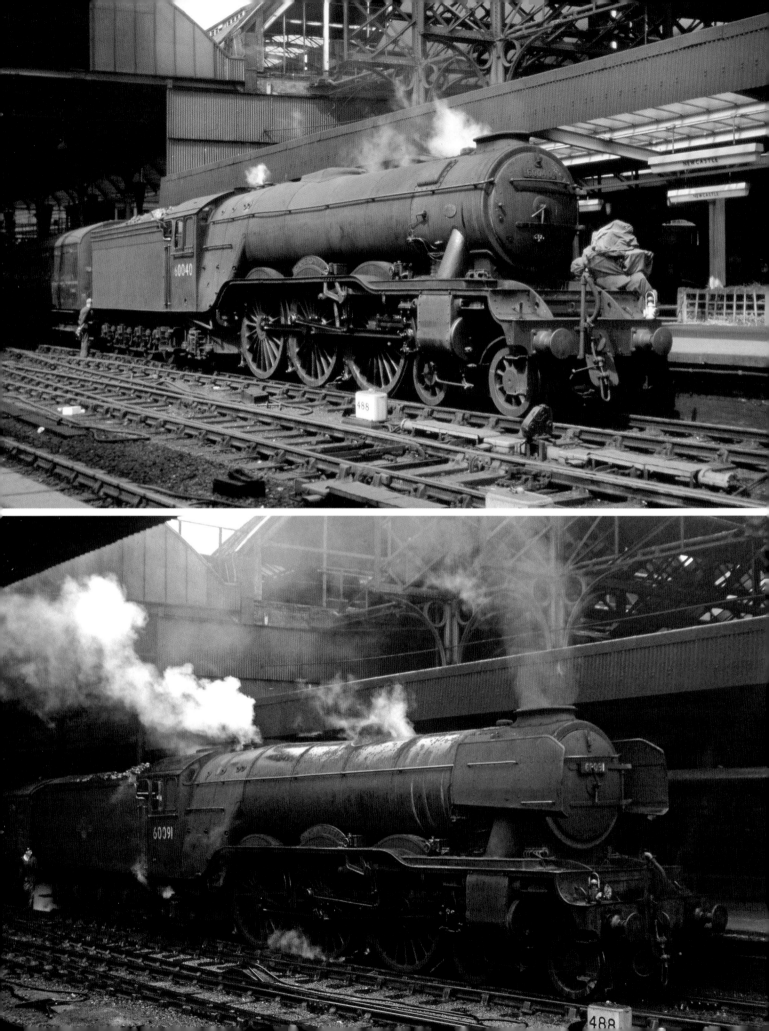

Above **No. 60039** *Sandwich*

No. 60039 *Sandwich* emerged to traffic from Doncaster Works during September 1934 with LNER non-corridor tender (5573) which was retained throughout its existence. All maintenance work was undertaken at Doncaster Works including adjustment to 75% cut-off by March, 1955; fitting double chimney and trough deflectors, July 1959 and June 1961 respectively. *Sandwich* was supplied with seven Diagram 94A boilers; two Diagram 94HP boilers; and two Diagram 107 boilers. Withdrawal was off King's Cross during March, 1963; cutting up at Doncaster Works. Photograph of *Sandwich* at King's Cross reproduced courtesy of the J.W. Armstrong Trust.

Opposite above **No. 60040** *Cameronian*

No. 60040 *Cameronian* is at Newcastle station with a double chimney fitted from October 16, 1959; trough deflectors were added March 24, 1962. After withdrawal from Gateshead on Monday July 6, 1964, *Cameronian* was sold for scrap to Hughes Bolckow, North Blyth during September of the same year. Photograph taken May 13, 1961 by H. Foster.

Opposite below **No 60091** *Captain Cuttle*

Work-stained no. 60091 *Captain Cuttle* waits to depart from Newcastle station on July 18, 1964. The engine was built as an A3, emerging from Doncaster Works during September, 1928. Repairs were carried out at Cowlairs Works and Doncaster Works until March 1949 when Doncaster Works had sole responsibility. Withdrawal was off Gateshead during October 1964; cutting up at A. Draper, Hull, later in that year. Photograph by David Christie.

Above **No. 60108** *Gay Crusader*

A side view shows no. 60108 *Gay Crusader* at Hitchin during 1961. Fitted to the rear crank pin is the connection for a Smith-Stone speed indicator which was acquired by the engine in the late 1950s. A similar scheme had been started before the Second World War and over 40 A1s and A3s had received one, but these were later removed during the conflict. No. 60108 was modified with the double chimney and trough deflectors in May, 1959 and November, 1961 respectively. Photograph reproduced courtesy of Ernie's Railway Archive.

Opposite **No. 60054** *Prince of Wales*

From entering service during December 1924 and until November 1926, the engine was named *Manna*. But from the latter date until withdrawal it carried the name *Prince of Wales* to commemorate a visit by the future King Edward VIII to Doncaster Works. All maintenance was carried out there, including: fitting long travel valves by December 1929; rebuilding to A3, July, 1943; conversion from right to left hand drive, December, 1953; fitting double chimney, August, 1958 and trough deflectors, May 1962. No. 60054 looks resplendent amidst the grime of King's Cross shed and the mechanical coaler, which was installed during major alterations implemented in the early 1930s. Photograph reproduced courtesy of Colourrail.

Below **No. 60037** *Hyperion*
Emerging as an A3, no. 2502, from Doncaster Works in July 1934, the engine's initial allocation was to Haymarket. Apart from a month at Carlisle Canal in 1954, *Hyperion* alternated between Haymarket and St Margarets sheds. The engine was the first A3 to be allocated to the latter in 1938 for use on Carlisle and Perth trains – no. 60037 is pictured in the Scottish city c. 1960. The double chimney was used from October 1958 and the trough deflectors would be added in May, 1962. Between 1934 and August 1941, *Hyperion* was attached to an LNER non-corridor tender; afterwards to three different GNR 5,000 gal. tenders, with the final one (no. 5276 – originally built with no. 2566 *Ladas* in April 1924) being in evidence here. Withdrawal was from St Margarets during December 1963. Scrapping was at Arnott Young, Carmyle in June of the following year. Photograph taken by Bill Reed.

Above **No. 60057 Ormonde**

No. 60057 *Ormonde* is at Galashiels on April 1st, 1961 with the 12.53 to Carlisle. Galashiels station was opened on November 1,1849 and closed on January 5, 1969. A new station opened on another site on September 6, 2015. Doncaster Works completed the building of *Ormonde*, as an A1, no. 2556, during February 1925 and the first allocation was to Grantham. Two years later the LNER began trials to determine the suitability of the A1s on the Waverley route but these proved fruitless and in 1928 A3s were allocated to Carlisle and achieved greater success on the difficult line. No. 2556 was not sent to Scotland until March 1939 when a berth was taken at Haymarket briefly before the engine relocated to St Margarets. *Ormonde* was a mainstay at Haymarket from April 1943 to later in April 1961 when staying for a short time at Carlisle Canal depot. No. 60057 was condemned at St Margarets during October, 1963 and cutting up was carried out at Arnott Young, Carmyle in June of the following year. Photograph by D.J. Dippie.

No. 60044 *Melton*

Speeding south of Retford at Eaton Wood with the Anglo Scottish Car Carrier is no. 60044 *Melton*. The train was a novel idea from British Railways and allowed holidaymakers to take their vehicles with them, even abroad as there was a connection to the ferries leaving the north-east ports. At the inauguration of the train the price of a ticket for two to Newcastle was £14 5s or a return to Edinburgh from King's Cross £32 10s. Photograph of *Melton* at Eaton Wood supplied by Colourrail.

Above No. 60109 *Hermit*

No. 60109 *Hermit* is adjacent to the King's Cross mechanical coaler during October, 1962. The engine had just undergone a Light Casual at Doncaster Works and this was the last work undertaken. *Hermit's* final allocation was to King's Cross extending from April, 1959 until December 29, 1962. Cutting up was at Doncaster Works, from April 1963. Photograph by Bill Reed.

Below No. 60108 *Gay Crusader*

During no. 60108 *Gay Crusader's* working life it was attached to four different GNR 5,000 gal. tenders as well as being supplied with five Diagram 94 boilers and seven Diagram 94A boilers. The engine was allocated six times to King's Cross and is seen here adjacent to King's Cross box. The last allocation was at Doncaster from September, 1963 until withdrawal during October, 1963. Photograph by Bill Reed.

Above **No. 60035** *Windsor Lad*

No. 60035 *Windsor Lad* is at Hawick on July 4, 1961. The engine returned to Haymarket in August, 1961 and there were no more works visits thereafter. Withdrawal was from Haymarket during September, 1961 followed by cutting up at Doncaster Works. Photograph taken by Bill Reed.

Above **No. 60100** *Spearmint*
Carlisle Kingmoor shed turntable was installed by the Caledonian Railway in 1903 and located at the south end of the facility, close to Etterby junction. No. 60100 *Spearmint* was photographed on the turntable in September 1964; the engine has probably travelled from Scotland with a goods service as it was allocated to Edinburgh St Margarets at this period. Photograph by Bill Reed.

Above **No. 60098** *Spion Kop*

No. 60098 *Spion Kop* is at Edinburgh Haymarket shed July 2, 1961. The open smokebox gives a glimpse of the Kylchap cowls contained within that caused such a dramatic improvement in the efficiency of the class. The cowls were developed by the Finnish engineer Kyösti Kylälä and were adopted for a new exhaust system designed by André Chapelon in the early 1920s. The main benefits were a more even draught through the boiler and reduced back pressure at the cylinders. Gresley first used the arrangement in 1934 on P2 no. 2001 *Cock o' the North* but after some difficulties reaching the optimum setting, coupled with high patent fees he did not stretch the application to other classes until 1937. Unfortunately a widespread adoption was delayed until the late 1950s and no. 60098 was a recipient in July 1959. Photograph by Bill Reed.

Above No. 60056 *Centenary*
All *Centenary*'s repairs and alterations were carried out at Doncaster Works and these included, fitting long travel valves from March, 1927; rebuilding to A3 August, 1944; adjustment to 75% cut-off, September, 1947; conversion from right to left hand drive, February 1954. *Centenary* was supplied with four Diagram 94 boilers and seven Diagram 94A boilers. Withdrawal was off Grantham during May, 1963 and cutting up at Doncaster Works. The photograph shows no. 60056 working an iron ore train at Grove Road on the East Coast Main Line between Gamston and Retford South and is reproduced courtesy of Ernie's Railway Archive.

Opposite above No. 60093 *Coronach*
No. 60093 Coronach pulls away from Riddings junction station, opened in March, 1862 , closed to passengers in June, 1964 and completely in January, 1967. Coronach had the Kylchap double chimney fitted in December, 1958. Although not fitted with trough deflectors, the locomotive had been involved in smoke deflecting experiments in 1931, with air entering the top of the smokebox and exiting behind the chimney. But, this arrangement was not adopted on this or any other locomotive in the class. *Coronach* was cut up at Doncaster Works. Photograph by Bill Reed.

Opposite below No. 60085 *Manna*
No. 60085 Manna approaches Calton Tunnel with empty stock for the Up afternoon 'Talisman'. Photograph by Eric Treacy from the David Joy collection.

Above **No. 60047** *Donovan*
An evocative shot of no. 60047 *Donovan* heading a northbound express at York station on August 13, 1962. The Grantham resident was soon to be moved on to Peterborough New England and was withdrawn there in April, 1963. Photograph by Richard Postill.

Opposite above **No. 60055** *Woolwinder*
In a view from Harringay West, facing north towards Hatfield and Hitchin, no. 60055 *Woolwinder* is heading the 08.47 Hull - King's Cross express on February 27, 1960. The engine was never fitted with trough deflectors. Photograph by Ben Brooksbank.

Opposite below **No 60087** *Blenheim*
Blenheim is pictured making a dramatic departure from Carlisle, passing Carlisle No. 1 signal box with the 13.28 slow train to Edinburgh via the Waverley Route in March, 1962. Withdrawal of *Blenheim* from Edinburgh St Margarets occurred during October, 1963. Scrapping was undertaken during June, 1964 by Arnott Young, Carmyle. Photograph by Peter Robinson.

Above No. 60083 *Sir Hugo*

No. 60083 *Sir Hugo* is seen hard at work on the Waverley Route during 1964. The engine was named – after the winner of the 1892 Derby – during November, 1925, just under a year after entering service. Initially, *Sir Hugo* went to traffic in the North Eastern Area at Heaton with both vacuum and Westinghouse brakes but the latter was removed in June, 1933. Withdrawal was from Gateshead during May, 1964; cutting up carried out at Hughes Bolckow, North Blyth. Photograph by Peter Robinson.

Opposite, above No. 60094 *Colorado*

No. 60094 *Colorado* approaches Stanley with the 08.25 Glasgow Buchanan Street to Aberdeen express during May, 1963. Towards the end of steam the Scottish Region wanted to speed up the principal expresses between the two cities using diesel traction. The units delivered turned out to be quite underpowered and unreliable. With the Eastern Region dieselisation scheme progressing swiftly and displacing locomotives that were still useful the ScR adopted a large number, mainly of the A4 Class, but also drafting in a couple of A3s – no. 60090 *Colombo* and no. 60094 *Colorado*. Both engines were allocated to Glasgow St Rollox shed and gave good accounts of themselves while employed there. Picture by Peter Robinson.

Opposite, below No. 60048 *Doncaster*

No. 60048 *Doncaster* passes through Hadley Wood on August 24, 1962. Rebuilding to A3 was carried out by May 16, 1946, a double chimney and trough deflectors fitted by May 29, 1959 and December 15, 1961. Withdrawal from Grantham was on Sunday September 8, 1963 and cutting up undertaken at Doncaster in September, 1963. Photograph from Ernie's Railway Archive.

Above **No. 60100** *Spearmint*

No. 60100 *Spearmint* is at Riccarton with the 14.00 Carlisle to Millerhill freight train during 1965. St Margarets was the locomotive's final shed before withdrawal in June, 1965. Cutting up was undertaken at Darlington Works. Photograph by Peter Robinson.

Below No. **60060** *The Tetrarch*

Brunswick Green livery was applied to no. 60060 from August 15, 1951 after a little over a 18 months in BR Blue. Soon afterwards conversion from right to left hand drive took place on September 4, 1953 and later a double chimney was fitted during March, 1959. *The Tetrarch* worked with three GNR tenders and two LNER streamlined non-corridor tenders; no. 5482, attached from July, 1943 to withdrawal, is seen here. The engine was also supplied with a Diagram 107 boiler – from A4 no. 60005 *Sir Charles Newton*. Withdrawal from Gateshead was during September, 1963 and scrapping took place a little later at Darlington Works. Photograph at Darlington station taken by John Arnott-Brown reproduced courtesy of the A1 Locomotive Trust.

Above No. **60077** *The White Knight*
Pulling away from Carlisle, past Stainton Junction, no. 60077 *The White Knight* is working a troop special from Barrow-in-Furness to Barry Links, routed from Carlisle to Edinburgh over the Waverley Route in July, 1961. Photograph by Peter Robinson.

Opposite above No. **60038** *Firdaussi*
No. 60038 *Firdaussi* is in charge of the 09.50 Edinburgh to St Pancras train – 'The Waverley' – and climbs away from Carlisle, past Duncowfold, during the Spring of 1961. Photograph by Peter Robinson.

Opposite below No. **60042** *Singapore*
Passing through Dunning with the 13.30 Aberdeen-Glasgow train is no. 60042 *Singapore*. Photograph by Peter Robinson.

Above **No. 60052 *Prince Palatine***

No. 60052 *Prince Palatine* has covered most of the long climb from Newcastleton to Whitrope as it approaches Riccarton Junction powering the 14.12 Carlisle Yard to Millerhill fully fitted-freight in June, 1965. The engine was maintained throughout its existence at Doncaster Works, but the final repairs were undertaken between May and August, 1965 at Darlington Works, a Light Casual (lasting 54 days) and Inverurie Works, an Unclassified (taking 24 days). *Prince Palatine* was allocated to St Margarets from August, 1963 until becoming the last A3 to be withdrawn in January, 1966. Photograph by Peter Robinson.

Opposite above and below **No. 60052 *Prince Palatine***

On June 5, 1965, no. 60052 *Prince Palatine* headed the Scottish Locomotive Preservation Fund Rail Tour. In the picture below on the opposite page the engine is departing from Edinburgh Waverley station and it worked through Newcastle-Hexham-Carlisle. On arrival at Carlisle it was declared a failure with a hotbox and A4 No 60027 *Merlin* was hastily sent for as a replacement. Opposite above, on the same day, no. 60052 is seen at Scotswood Bridge. The top photograph is reproduced courtesy of the J.W.Armstrong Trust and the one below by courtesy of Simon Lathlane.

Above No. 60098 *Spion Kop*

On withdrawal from St Margarets on October 28, 1963, no. 60098 *Spion Kop* was moved to Inverurie Works for cutting up. The engine is pictured here during that process. Photograph reproduced courtesy of Colourrail.

Opposite above No. 60051 *Blink Bonny*

On April 16, 1964, no. 60051 *Blink Bonny* is pictured during a two-hour pause at Derby Midland railway station whilst heading 'The South Yorkshireman No. 2' organised by the Halifax Railfans & Pennine Railway Society. Starting at Sowerby Bridge, the 'special' ran via Brighouse, Huddersfield, Mirfield, Thornhill Junction, Royston, Cudworth, Sheffield, Derby, Stoke and Crewe. The return journey took in Stockport Edgeley, Rochdale, Sowerby Bridge, Brighouse and ended at Huddersfield. Locomotive no. 42411 was used on the outward journey between Sowerby Bridge and Huddersfield; no. 60051 for the remainder of the trip. *Blink Bonny* was only supplied with two tenders: one GNR 5,000 gal; and an LNER non-corridor. A double chimney and trough deflectors were fitted, August, 1959 and March, 1962. After undergoing a Light repair at Gorton during December, 1924, the engine was maintained afterwards at Doncaster Works. Withdrawal was from Gateshead on Monday November 23, 1964, after 40 years and 11 days in service. Scrapping was at Hughes Bolckow, North Blyth. Photograph reproduced courtesy of Paul Braybrook.

Opposite below No 60068 *Sir Visto*

Withdrawn off Carlisle Canal during August 1962, no 60068 *Sir Visto* was cut up at Doncaster Works, seen here, during August 1962. The works' scrapyard dismantled 36 members of the class, while the others went to: Inverurie Works two; Cowlairs Works one; A. Draper, Hull, eight; Henderson's, Airdrie, one; Arnott Young, nine; Hughes Bolckow, four; Darlington Works, nine; Motherwell Machinery & Scrap, one; R.A. King, Norwich, six; P.W. McLellan, Langloan, one.

Flying Scotsman

No. 60103 *Flying Scotsman* was withdrawn off
King's Cross on Tuesday, January 15, 1963. The last
BR service run was on the previous day, working
the 13.15 King's Cross-Leeds service as far as
Doncaster. The engine had travelled approx.
2,076,000 miles. An agreement to purchase the
locomotive, was made between BR and
businessman Alan Pegler. *Flying Scotsman* was the
first main line express locomotive ever to be
purchased with the intention of being kept
running. The engine was put through Doncaster
Works for restoration. *Flying Scotsman* then worked
a number of Special trains. Opposite, Alan Pegler is
seen at Marylebone Station on April 18, 1964
when *Flying Scotsman* arrived on a SLS Great
Central special. photograph by David Christie.

Below *Flying Scotsman* is outside Doncaster Works' Paint
Shop after restoration during 1963. The work undertaken
included removing the Kylchap double blast pipe, double
chimney and smoke deflectors. Refitted was a single blast pipe
and single chimney. The LNER Apple Green livery was
applied along with the number 4472. The engine remained as
an A3 and was coupled to a corridor tender that was formerly
paired with ex-A4 60034 *Lord Faringdon*.

Left From November, 1968 to February, 1969 *Flying Scotsman* underwent an overhaul at Hunslet Works, Leeds. The work included a boiler re-tube. On February 2, 1969, steam locomotive enthusiast, the Bishop of Wakefield, Dr Eric Treacy, spent brief but happy off-duty minutes examining the locomotive at close quarters. Dr Treacy once travelled from York to Edinburgh on the footplate of *Flying Scotsman*. Photograph, *Yorkshire Post Newspapers*.

Below *Flying Scotsman* is at Doncaster Works in 1969 after undergoing a Light overhaul prior to being shipped from Liverpool to Boston, USA to begin a tour. This was undertaken as a trade mission with the endorsement of Prime Minister Harold Wilson. For the trip *Flying Scotsman* was fitted with a bell and cow catcher. A second tender holding 6,000 gallons of water only was acquired during late 1966. It formerly belonged to A4 no. 60009 *Union of South Africa*.

Above Early in 1973, *Flying Scotsman* was purchased by Hon. (later Sir) William McAlpine and returned to England. By September, after a Light overhaul at Derby, the engine was undertaking commercial runs once again, the first one between Newport and Shrewsbury. A highlight for the engine in 1978 was appearing in the film 'Agatha' alongside Vanessa Redgrave and Dustin Hoffman. Also in 1978, *Flying Scotsman* was present at Doncaster Plant Works' Railex 125 held in June of that year. This celebrated 125 years of the Works' existence and visitors to the event are waiting to climb into the engine's cab.

Opposite top Depicted are the driver (left) and fireman (right) who accompanied *Flying Scotsman* to the US. Although members of the crew were provided by BR, they were paid for by Alan Pegler. The entourage included a nine-coach train and carried trade stands from Britain's prominent export companies. The tour across eastern and Southern USA was a success covering 2,251 miles and made a profit. *Flying Scotsman* was stored at Staton, Texas for the Winter.

Opposite below From June to October 1970, *Flying Scotsman* toured mid-USA and Canada until being stored over the winter in Toronto. In 1971 the engine travelled to San Francisco where the entire adventure ran out of cash. Alan Pegler returned to England to file for bankruptcy, while *Flying Scotsman* was stored at Sharpe Army Base, Stockton, Sacaramento for safekeeping. No. 4472 is depicted running on Jefferson Street, San Francisco during March, 1972. Photograph reproduced courtesy of Drew Jacksich.

Above There was a change in *Flying Scotsman*'s ownership in February, 1996 with Tony Marchington buying the engine at a cost of £1,250, 000. A major overhaul, started during the previous year, was then resumed. A 'Flying Scotsman' Association was formed with Alan Pegler becoming the President. Over the weekend of July 26/27, 2003, Wabtec Rail Ltd organised celebrations to mark Doncaster Plant Works' 150 years of existence. Naturally *Flying Scotsman* was present but in a hybrid appearance, with trough deflectors, painted in LNER Apple Green livery and carrying the 4472 number. The engine was displayed near the Doncaster Works' New Erecting shop from where it had emerged in 1923. Alongside were other well-known favourite Doncaster-built and serviced engines including V2 *Green Arrow* and A4s *Mallard* and *Union of South Africa*. *Flying Scotsman* is pictured with stewards and police who were involved in the 150th Anniversary event.

Opposite above Initally, after returning from the US, *Flying Scotsman*'s first home depot was at Market Overton but then in August, 1974 a move was made to Steamtown, Carnforth. For a number of years, the engine participated in several prestigious events including the 1975 Stockton & Darlington Anniversary celebrations. The engine is alongside Carnforth's giant cast-concrete coal stage on July 5, 1984.

Opposite below In 1988 *Flying Scotsman* made another foreign trip; this time to Australia. Whilst in the country no. 4472 broke the world non-stop steam record of 422 miles. The journey, Parkes to Broken Hill, included 297 miles of straight track. Taking 9 hours and 25 minutes with 535 tons gross, the record-breaking run saw seven British and Australian drivers being used. Following its return to Britain, the engine continued to delight crowds up and down the country. In 1993, Pete Waterman became joint owner of the locomotive with Sir William McAlpine. An overhaul from April to July, 1993 saw the locomotive change appearance. Amongst other parts, it was fitted with smoke deflectors, a Kylchap double blast pipe and chimney. The livery applied was BR Green and the running number changed to 60103. *Flying Scotsman* is at Llangollen station on March 17, 1994. Photograph by Bill Reed.

Tony Marchington's ownership of *Flying Scotsman* and attempts to develop it as a brand name lasted until bankruptcy in late 2003. The locomotive was put up for sale, with the National Railway Museum purchasing it for around £2.5 million supported by a £1.8 million grant from the National Heritage Lottery Fund and the generosity of the public. *Flying Scotsman* was employed for a year on charter trains before failing and withdrawn for repairs towards the end of 2005. Thereafter, the locomotive underwent a protracted and expensive overhaul. Much of the work was initially carried out at the NRM in their own workshops and later at Ian Riley & Son's workshops in Bury. The overhaul was completed in January, 2016 and the entire restoration project has cost in the region of £4.2m, again with the help of the Heritage Lottery Fund. This has brought *Flying Scotsman* back to life, resplendent in BR Brunswick Green livery, and with number 60103. Testing of the engine started on the East Lancashire Railway on January 8, 2016 and the first main line run, pulling the 'Winter Cumbrian Mountain Express' from Carnforth to Carlisle, took place on February 6, 2016. An inaugural journey from London King's Cross to York ran on February 25, 2016. Pictures on the opposite page of the engine undergoing restoration at the NRM were taken on December 1, 2009 by Hugh Parkin. The one above of *Flying Scotsman* running on the initial King's Cross - York outing was taken at Arksey, near Doncaster, by Neil Daykin.

Index of A3s

Also available from Great Northern by Peter Tuffrey

The Last Days of Scottish Steam

The Last Years of Yorkshire Steam

visit *www.greatnorthernbooks.co.uk* for details.